Developing Your Teaching

Developing Your Teaching engages you in a dialogue that both supports and challenges you in developing your teaching. Focusing on the *processes* involved in this, and the *practical actions* that you can take, it encourages a continuous approach to development, seeking insight and inspiration to underpin the process. Through a blend of ideas, interactive review points and case study examples from university teachers, the book unfolds as an accessible handbook for professional practice and provides ideas on a range of topics including:

- choosing effective teaching practices
- learning from student feedback and peer review
- working with others
- mentoring
- carrying out development projects
- undertaking specific roles that involve the development of teaching.

Developing Your Teaching will be particularly helpful for new lecturers, tutors and graduate teaching assistants. Experienced staff involved in ongoing professional development for their teaching will also benefit, as this book is for everyone who would like to think more deeply about their teaching.

Peter Kahn is Senior Professional Development Adviser at the University of Manchester, where he works with a range of staff whose interests are in the development of education. His earlier books include the co-edited *A Guide to Staff and Educational Development* and *Effective Learning and Teaching in Mathematics and its Applications*, both now from Routledge.

Lorraine Walsh is the Director of Academic Professional Development at the University of Dundee, and her main interests are in continuing professional development and the professional identity of university teachers.

Key Guides for Effective Teaching in Higher Education Series

Edited by Kate Exley

This indispensable series is aimed at new lecturers, postgraduate students who have teaching time, graduate teaching assistants, part-time tutors and demonstrators, as well as experienced teaching staff who may feel it is time to review their skills in teaching and learning.

Titles in this series will provide the teacher in higher education with practical, realistic guidance on the various different aspects of their teaching role, which is underpinned not only by current research in the field, but also by the extensive experience of individual authors, with a keen eye kept on the limitations and opportunities therein. By bridging a gap between academic theory and practice, all titles will provide generic guidance on teaching, learning and assessment issues which is then brought to life through the use of short illustrative examples drawn from a range of disciplines. All titles in this series will:

- represent up-to-date thinking and incorporate the use of communication and information technologies (C&IT) where appropriate;
- consider methods and approaches for teaching and learning when there is an increasing diversity in learning and a growth in student numbers;
- encourage reflective practice and self-evaluation, and a means of developing the skills of teaching, learning and assessment;
- provide links and references to further work on the topic and research evidence where appropriate.

Titles in the series will prove invaluable whether they are used for self-study or as part of a formal induction programme on teaching in higher education, and will also be of relevance to teaching staff working in further education settings.

Other titles in this series:

Assessing Skills and Practice
– Sally Brown and Ruth Pickford

Assessing Students' Written Work: Marking Essays and Reports
– Catherine Haines

Designing Learning: From Module Outline to Effective Teaching
– Chris Butcher, Clara Davies and Melissa Highton

Developing Your Teaching: Ideas, Insight and Action
– Peter Kahn and Lorraine Walsh

Giving a Lecture: From Presenting to Teaching
– Kate Exley and Reg Dennick

Small Group Teaching
– Kate Exley and Reg Dennick

Using C&IT to Support Teaching
– Paul Chin

Developing Your Teaching

Ideas, insight and action

Peter Kahn
and
Lorraine Walsh

LONDON AND NEW YORK

First published 2006
by Routledge
2 Park Square, Milton Park, Abingdon, Oxon OX14 4RN

Simultaneously published in the USA and Canada
by Routledge
270 Madison Avenue, New York, NY 10001

Routledge is an imprint of the Taylor & Francis Group, an informa business

Typeset in Times by
Florence Production Ltd, Stoodleigh, Devon
Printed and bound in Great Britain by
TJ International, Padstow, Cornwall

British Library Cataloguing in Publication Data
A catalogue record for this book is available from
the British Library

Library of Congress Cataloging in Publication Data
Kahn, Peter, 1967–
Developing your teaching: ideas, insight and action / Peter
Kahn and Lorraine Walsh.
p. cm.
Includes bibliographical references and index.
1. College teaching. 2. Learning. I. Walsh, Lorraine.
II. Title.
LB2331.K245 2006
378.1′2–dc22 2005031468

ISBN10: 0–415–37272–0 (hbk)
ISBN10: 0–415–37273–9 (pbk)

ISBN13: 978–0–415–37272–5 (hbk)
ISBN13: 978–0–415–37273–2 (pbk)

Contents

Illustrations

FIGURES

TABLES

CASE STUDIES

Foreword

As soon as I began to read this book, I felt as if a close friend was taking me through one important educational topic after another – and it seemed as if one writer, and not two, was doing that. This almost avuncular friend offered me advice and suggestions in a thoughtful and thought-provoking way that left me feeling that I had profited from each chapter, from each exchange between us. It was only when I finished reading that it dawned on me that this was supposed to be a book directed first of all towards readers who are relatively new to university teaching. What a wonderful ability the writers have displayed, then, in managing without apparent effort to be as useful and interesting to an old greybeard such as me as they will undoubtedly prove to the next generation of university teachers!

How have they managed to cater effectively for such a wide readership? I am sure part of their secret lies in the way they have commissioned, edited and used to pertinent effect what they call case studies, but which to me are succinct and telling cameos. The brevity of these short accounts focuses the reader on the message that may matter to them in the encapsulated piece of experience, and that can be drawn upon, or even pillaged. It also helps avoid the danger that a reader may shrug off a longer account with the disparaging 'This is fine, but it's not in my discipline!' These cameos effectively introduce and then reinforce and explain important and generalisable points in the main text; they also provide many useful and practical suggestions in so doing.

The result is a text that avoids the style and tone of so many, no doubt worthy, books in this market that are aimed nowadays at new recruits to the teaching profession in higher education. Here you will find no watered-down coverage of theories and research, which might leave you feeling somewhat patronised as well as slightly overwhelmed and inadequate. Instead the writers present their rationale for each topic in their coverage with what I tended to assimilate as reasoned arguments – exemplified and substantiated by these short cameos or case studies, and with due reference to the experts throughout. Their wise choice of references is provided for the benefit of those who wish to delve deeper, although the text on its own will be self-sufficient for many first-time teachers making a start in this demanding profession.

The writers also work unobtrusively, but effectively, at encouraging active learning on the part of the reader. I have never been a great enthusiast for in-text questions in textbooks – apparently patronising questions that seem to expect me to find a piece of paper and write down my responses. I did not ever feel that these writers were going to be disappointed if I failed to respond in that way; yet I knew, somehow, that they expected me to *think* about their questions – and I certainly did so, and did so profitably, as far as I was concerned.

Even the grouping of topics in the various chapters conveys a message to the reader, as well as saying something important about the writers and their values. In the early chapters we are taken straightaway into issues of motivation for teaching, the value of adopting an objective and systematic approach to the way we plan our teaching, and to a sharing with and by the writers of their own enthusiasm for a task, which has sometimes been downplayed in these research-conscious years, yet can be so rewarding in its turn. Tellingly, then, they next take us on to how we can review whatever teaching we are already planning and presenting and to how we can learn and develop and profit from that review. 'Bravo', I found myself exclaiming when I reached that point, for formative evaluation still tends to be a somewhat neglected topic in higher educational circles, yet it can so often be the cost-effective springboard from which developments – and fulfilment – originate.

The next switch of emphasis is welcome, appropriate – but again perhaps slightly unusual in this type of text. We are encouraged to think, and to think constructively, about working with others, about using mentors, about harnessing the potential of critical friends, and above all about creating effective support networks, which we will undoubtedly need and from which we can profit greatly. The days of individual teaching are well behind us; we do well to think (as we are encouraged to do here) in terms of communities of learning and collaborative approaches to our teaching.

It is clear, by this point in their text, that these writers are encouraging us – effectively – to think in terms of advancing the quality of our teaching and of our students' learning experiences, in the present climate where so much development has taken place in recent years, and where the pace of development and enhancement continues to accelerate. They follow up that encouragement with thorough, and again practical, advice and suggestions about our engagement in pedagogical and action research, leading into a general discussion of the scholarship of learning and teaching and how we can and should relate to it.

If I had a friend or relative who was entering higher education as a teacher, I could think of no more suitable mentor to inspire, advise, encourage and sustain them than the duo who have written this rather exceptional book. I do hope that you, who have borrowed or purchased it, will find as much inspiration, sound common sense, reasoned rationale and exemplars of sound practice as I have already done – and will undoubtedly continue to do when I re-read it, as I shall certainly do.

John Cowan
Author of *On Becoming an Innovative University Teacher*
(second edition, Society for Research into Higher
Education and Open University Press,
Buckingham, 2006)

Series preface

This series of books grew out of discussions with new lecturers and part-time teachers in universities and colleges who were keen to develop their teaching skills. However, experienced colleagues may also enjoy and find merit in the books, particularly the discussions about current issues that are impacting on teaching and learning in further and higher education, e.g. widening participation, disability legislation and the integration of C&IT in teaching.

New lecturers are now likely to be required by their institutions to take part in teaching development programmes. This frequently involves attending workshops, investigating teaching through mini-projects and reflecting on their practice. Many teaching programmes ask participants to develop their own teaching portfolios and to provide evidence of their developing skills and understanding. Scholarship of teaching is usually an important aspect of the teaching portfolio. New teachers can be asked to consider their own approach to teaching in relation to the wider literature, research findings, and theory of teaching and learning. However, when people are beginning their teaching careers a much more pressing need may be to design and deliver an effective teaching session for tomorrow. Hence, the intention of this series is to provide a complementary mix of very practical teaching tips and guidance, together with a strong basis and clear rationale for their use.

In many institutions the numbers of part-time and occasional teachers actually outnumber the full-time staff. Yet the provision of formal training and development for part-time teachers is more sporadic and variable across the sector. As a result, this diverse group of educators can feel isolated and left out of the updating and support offered to their full-time counterparts. Never has there been so many part-time teachers involved in the design and delivery of courses, the support and guidance of students, and the monitoring and assessment of learning. The group includes the thousands of postgraduate students who work as laboratory demonstrators, problem-class tutors, project supervisors and class teachers. The group includes clinicians, lawyers and professionals who contribute their specialist knowledge and skills to enrich the learning experience for many vocational and professional course students. The group also includes the many hourly paid and jobbing tutors who have helped full-time staff to cope with the expansion and diversification of further and higher education.

Universities sometimes struggle to know how many part-time staff they employ to teach and, as a group, occasional teachers are notoriously difficult to contact systematically through university and college communication systems. Part-time and occasional teachers often have other roles and responsibilities, and teaching is a small but important part of what they do each day. Many part-time tutors would not expect to undertake the full range of teaching activities of full-time staff, but may well do lots of tutoring or lots of class teaching but never lecture or supervise (or vice versa). So the series provides short practical books that focus squarely on different teaching roles and activities. The first four books published are:

- *Assessing Students' Written Work: Marking Essays and Reports*
- *Giving a Lecture: From Presenting to Teaching*
- *Small Group Teaching*
- *Using C&IT to Support Teaching*

The books are all very practical with detailed discussion of teaching techniques and methods, but they are based on educational theory and research findings. Articles are referenced, further readings and related web sites are given, and workers in the field are quoted and acknowledged. To this end Dr George Brown has been commissioned to produce an associated web-based guide on student learning which can be freely accessed by readers to accompany the books and provide a substantial foundation for the teaching and assessment practices discussed and recommended for the texts.

There is much enthusiasm and support here too for the excellent work currently being carried out by the Higher Education Academy subject centres within discipline groupings (indeed, individual subject centres are suggested as sources of further information throughout these volumes). The need to provide part-time tutors with realistic connections with their own disciplines is keenly felt by all the authors in the series and 'how it might work in your department' examples are given at the end of many of the activity-based chapters. However, there is no doubt some merit in sharing teaching developments across the boundaries of disciplines, culture and country as many of the problems in the tertiary education sector are themselves widely shared.

UNDERLYING THEMES

The use of Communications and Information Technology (C&IT) to enrich student learning and to help manage the workload of teachers is a recurring theme in the series. I acknowledge that not all teachers may yet have access to state-of-the-art teaching resources and facilities. However, the use of virtual learning environments, e-learning provision and audio-visual presentation media is now widespread in universities.

The books also acknowledge and try to help new teachers respond to the growing and changing nature of the student population. Students with non-traditional backgrounds, international students, students who have disabilities or special needs are encouraged through the government's widening participation agenda to take part in further and higher education. The books seek to advise teachers on current legislative requirements and offer guidance on recommended good practice on teaching diverse groups of students.

These were our goals and I and my co-authors sincerely hope these volumes prove to be a helpful resource for colleagues, both new and experienced, in further and higher education.

Acknowledgements

We are grateful to Helen Pritt and staff at Routledge for their roles in bringing this book to publication, and also to our Series Editor, Kate Exley, for her vision behind the series and for prompting this book itself. We further appreciate John Cowan for contributing the Foreword.

We would like to say a special thank you to Gaye Manwaring for providing material, ideas and inspiration on the action-oriented evaluation tools in Chapter 4; and also to Jim Petch and David Baume for ideas on project management techniques, and to Peter Hartley and Bob Rotherham for providing material on teaching portfolios.

This book benefits significantly from the case studies. We are thus particularly grateful to all those who have contributed in this way. We have also appreciated comments that case study authors have made on the text of their chapter(s). On this note, thanks are also due to Kate Day, Ruth Pilkington and others for comments on specific chapters.

Many thanks, finally, to the colleagues, friends and family who have been inspirational, supportive and encouraging in equal measure.

Chapter 1

The beginning of development

Perplexity is the beginning of knowledge.

(Kahlil Gibran)

Why develop your teaching? As university teachers we are also learners, and the process of learning about our teaching is a never-ending story of inspiration, ideas and action. Developing our practice can mean improved effectiveness but it must mean more to us than increased efficiency. It might result in better evaluation scores but it should also mean enhanced student learning. This book is for everyone who would like to think more deeply about their teaching. More than that, it is a book for individuals who want to change their practice and to continue to develop as professionals.

The focus of this book is on *developing* your teaching. The aim here is not to present an end point or an ideal vision to which you might aspire; no such thing exists outwith the realms of fantasy. Rather, we focus on the processes of developing your teaching, and the practical actions that you can take within your own professional context.

Working in today's mass higher education system means operating within a constantly changing field of practice. These changes can come in the form of technological innovations, for example, with the development of online learning communities and interactive teaching tools; or through national initiatives, such as widening participation and access to higher education; or legislative change, which may have a diverse rather than uniform impact. The tertiary education system is also an area where adopting a positive and thoughtful approach towards your teaching may be viewed as an ambiguous career move in a climate apparently ruled both politically and economically by the research assessment exercise and the pressures to publish – and to keep on publishing.

Yet the emphasis needs to be on managing more creatively the research imperative, and associated trends in learning and teaching, rather than abandoning all before it. In our professional practice, learning and development are integral parts of all of the roles we play as both teachers and researchers; and also as scholars. For Boyer (1990: 16), this idea of scholarship is not only 'engaging in original research' but 'also stepping back from one's investigation, looking for connections, building bridges between theory and practice, and communicating one's knowledge effectively': a holistic approach to our practice, within which teaching forms an integral part.

As well as responding to this external environment, we need to be inspired, enthused and motivated to develop our practice. So, before we begin to look at what this book can offer you, take a few minutes to think about what you can offer yourself. Think about the following question and consider what your response tells you about yourself as a teacher and your approach to developing your practice.

My attitude to developing my teaching is:

- maintaining competence
- eagerly seeking new approaches
- ongoing development
- doing enough to get by.

Do you grasp every development opportunity with both hands or do you wait to be prompted by others to engage with the idea of improving your practice? Are you the kind of person who wants to continue to grow and develop as a person and as a professional or are you happy feeling that you are doing 'just enough'? Are you content to be this kind of person, this kind of professional?

When we begin to think about developing our practice we can feel perplexed: by the attitudes of our students, the reactions of our colleagues or the requirements of our institution. There can appear to be many more questions than answers. Sometimes this is stimulating and motivating, but it can also prove to be a turn-off from development activities and you might feel that it is better to stick with the tried and tested methods: if it ain't broke don't fix it. Yet, as professional university teachers we have ownership of and responsibility for our professional development. Eraut (1987, cited in Cole and Knowles, 2000: 12) identified four models of teacher professional development – the defect model, the change model, the problem-solving model and the growth model – which reflect the history of approaches and attitudes towards professional development. The four models trace the movement from an externally directed approach towards greater personal ownership of the process. The final stage, or growth model, facilitates a 'continuous process of professional growth through inquiry, interaction and reflection'.

This introductory chapter is designed to encourage you to engage with this book in a way that draws on this more continuous approach to your own development. In the next section we outline the main ideas that we cover, helping you to access the elements of the book that are currently the most relevant to you. If we are to develop our teaching in an ongoing fashion, we also need insight and inspiration to underpin the process, otherwise we soon tire of change. A further section both encourages you to consider how you personally seek this insight and addresses how we have sought to build sources of inspiration into this book. Our final section reminds us that this book is designed to prompt actual changes in your practice, and it again introduces ways in which we support this. Unless your practice moves on, there will certainly be little reason to engage regularly in development processes.

IDEAS

> The beginning is the most important part of the work.
>
> (Plato)

We aim in this book to provide you with a variety of ideas, including those that relate to working with and learning from others; that focus on specific aspects of your practice; and that involve you evaluating both who you are as a teacher and the ways in which your practice is developing. Before we outline the ideas that this book offers, we would like to encourage you to think about your own sources of ideas for developing your practice. With a greater awareness of your own approaches, you will be better placed to select from among our proposals. Think about the following statements and select those that match best with your approach to your practice. What do your responses say about you as a university teacher?

Stimulation for developing my teaching practice comes from:

- picking up ideas as and when I notice them
- being advised what to work on
- actively seeking better ways of working
- working with others.

Do you pick up ideas from team-teaching or sharing experiences with colleagues? Perhaps you prefer to work on your own, seeking out articles or books for information and new ideas. Maybe you teach in the way that you were taught, perhaps emulating a favourite lecturer or tutor, and you have not considered making any changes to that approach. Consider in that case how you will be able to respond to the changing higher education system. How will you deal with the changing student population that has resulted from widening participation and inclusion strategies? Or how will you fit within an education system geared to rapid technological advance, inter-professional working and innovation?

We want to work with you in this book to develop a range of strategies and approaches that can support you in creating the personal and professional knowledge you need in order to develop your day-to-day teaching practice in the face of this changing educational climate. In Chapter 2 we make a start on this process by looking at choosing effective teaching approaches. We begin by asking you to consider your own experiences. A good deal of richness and potential can come from learning derived directly from your teaching. Such emergent learning arises from your own practice in the course of your everyday activities, and is rooted in, drawn from and based upon that experience. It comes from being more attuned to what Mason (2002) calls 'the discipline of noticing'.

Emergent learning (Megginson, 1994) is an authentic approach to developing your teaching that involves drawing from your own experiences and focuses clearly on improving and developing your own practice. As a result, your learning 'emerges' from what you do in your everyday teaching rather than being 'brought in' as the result of external influences. In this way you intentionally and deliberately build learning into your practice. Knowledge about your teaching develops, is tested, reviewed and refined through iterative cycles that lead to the emergence of deeper understanding. We should not restrict ourselves to our own ideas only, however, and the chapter moves on to discuss how you might draw ideas from other sources in order to develop your practice, such as evidence from theory and evidence from research.

We hope to make you enthusiastic about developing your practice, and Chapter 3 considers inspiration for teaching. A central aspect of this inspirational approach is making connections – with your subject, your students and your colleagues, as well as with your own inner world. We also want to encourage you to experiment with your teaching: to take action, review, reflect and absorb. In Chapter 4 we discuss the ways in which you can begin to appraise your teaching practice through self-evaluation. This chapter takes a two-part approach to looking at self-evaluation, including the why, what and how of evaluating one's practice and also suggesting a number of tools that you might use to support self-evaluation.

Eraut's (1994: 13) learning professional 'relies on three main sources: publications in a variety of media; practical experience; and people'. We invite you to engage with your colleagues in dialogue, debate and collaborative working. In Chapters 5 and 6 we look at learning from, and working with, others and the ways in which you can begin to develop this aspect of your practice. We can learn from both students and colleagues in a variety of ways, but we have chosen to look specifically at two aspects on which you can begin to build as a regular part of your teaching practice: student feedback and peer observation. Collaborative approaches to developing your teaching – networking, communities of practice and working in a team – are also considered in some detail, while in Chapter 7 we look at mentoring as a specific way of working with a colleague, or colleagues, in developing your teaching.

Refreshing and enlivening your teaching are essential in order to keep both you and your students motivated and engaged in the teaching and learning process. In Chapter 8 we encourage you to consider introducing new developments into your teaching and also to begin thinking about researching your teaching practice. Researching our own teaching can support our development in a number of ways, including the refining of professional judgement and skills, encouraging us to consider our academic practice from a holistic standpoint and, perhaps most importantly, providing us with greater insight into student learning.

In Chapter 9 we consider the challenges and opportunities inherent in taking on a new role within your teaching practice. Adopting such a role can prove to be exciting and rewarding, but it is also worth reflecting on the proverb 'The person who thinks he is leading but has no followers is merely taking a stroll'. Gaining support and confidence from your colleagues takes more than simply being appointed in a leadership position. Building positive and effective relationships is a key part of that process and links directly to the topics of several of the preceding chapters, including working with, and learning from, others. Finally, Chapter 10 draws together the key components of our dialogue with you, the reader. It aims to support you in deciding upon the choices you will make over the direction of your development. Discovering what works for you and situating this within your own personal story is an important part of shaping the development of your teaching.

INSIGHTS

> We cannot separate our sense of Self from our experiences.
>
> (Patricia Cranton, 2001)

How can we gain further and deeper insight into our practice? Ideas are a good starting point from which to develop our teaching. Yet we often need something more in order to encourage us to try out the teaching strategies we have heard about or to consider putting into practice the examples we have read about in the literature. We need to be inspired. Do you feel that your own teaching is a source of inspiration? Or that of your colleagues? Consider the following suggestions and think about which of the statements best reflects your practice.

My teaching is a source of:

- opportunity
- income
- anxiety
- inspiration.

Do you see your teaching practice as an opportunity to try out new things and to develop and enrich that aspect of your academic work? Are you inspired by what you do? Or does the thought of your teaching raise more concerns than satisfaction for you? Is it an aspect of being an academic that you feel simply comes with the territory, rather than being a source of enjoyment or an area for development in its own right?

Actively seeking out inspiration for your teaching can help you to view your teaching practice in a new light and from a fresh perspective. Real examples of the ways in which theoretical ideas, suggestions or strategies can work in practice are an excellent way in which to achieve this and can help you to gain insight into how those approaches might work for you in developing your teaching. In this book we aim to provide you with that inspiration through the inclusion of authentic case studies from practice.

Each of the case studies has been provided by colleagues working currently in higher education. Their personal stories originate from a range of discipline areas and are drawn from the UK and from other countries, including Spain, Denmark and Saudi Arabia. The individual examples demonstrate a range of approaches to developing teaching, such as addressing challenges, exploring issues through personal narratives and adopting a variety of approaches including team teaching, mentoring and collaborative working in order to develop practice.

The case studies provide examples of development in action. While each example reflects the personal experience of one individual, or sometimes a group of colleagues, the experiences they discuss, the approaches they use and the learning that they demonstrate can act as triggers or prompts for you actively to begin to develop your own teaching. Use the case studies to gain insight into ways in which those ideas, activities or approaches might work for you in developing your own practice. Be inspired. Look for insights into developing your own teaching: and take action.

ACTION

> It is our attitude at the beginning of a difficult task which, more than anything else, will affect its successful outcome.
>
> (William James)

Reading about, thinking about and reflecting on your academic practice are all positive steps towards developing your teaching. However, these are all essentially passive activities. In order to make a positive impact on your practice, developing your teaching must result from a conscious decision. Genuine development, enhancement and enrichment of academic practice involve pushing the boundaries of your comfort zone, challenging your assumptions and taking positive steps towards change. Are you up to this challenge?

Begin to think about this by evaluating your practice in relation to the statements below. Consider how your current attitude and approach to your teaching practice affects the way you teach now and the ways in which your practice might develop in the future.

My response to suggestions for changing the way I teach is:

- sticking with the tried and tested
- trying things out for myself
- if it ain't broke – don't fix it
- considering and reflecting upon a range of options.

Are you the kind of person who embraces new opportunities and adopts a proactive approach to developing your teaching? Do you view this kind of development as an integral part of your work as an academic? Or do you find yourself struggling to make changes or perhaps reluctant to take that first step? Is this how you view your future career? If so, it is at risk of becoming stale and tired before it has even begun.

Gaining the confidence, ideas, enthusiasm and strategies to make positive changes to your practice takes work. It also needs to be planned, supported and structured in a way that works for you. Throughout this book we introduce you to a range of practical tools, strategies and prompts for action that can help you to begin to think about ways of developing your teaching; and we encourage you to take time to pause and work through the short review activities that can be found throughout the book to help you structure your thinking about developing your teaching, and to provide a realistic basis for subsequent action. In this way we hope to be able to support you in taking that first step – and many more.

REFERENCES

Boyer, E. L. (1990) *Scholarship Reconsidered: Priorities of the Professoriate*. San Francisco, CA: Carnegie Foundation/Jossey-Bass.

Cole, A. and Knowles, J. G. (2000) *Researching Teaching. Exploring Teacher Development Through Reflexive Inquiry*. Needham Heights, MA: Allyn & Bacon.

Cranton, P. (2001) *Becoming an Authentic Teacher in Higher Education*. Malabar, FL: Krieger.

Eraut, M. (1987) 'Inservice Teacher Education', in Dunkin, M. (ed.), *The International Encyclopedia of Teaching and Teacher Education*. New York: Pergamon Press.

Eraut, M. (1994) *Developing Professional Knowledge and Competence*. London: Falmer Press.

Mason, J. (2002) *Researching Your Own Practice: The Discipline of Noticing*. London: RoutledgeFalmer.

Megginson, D. (1994) 'Planned and Emergent Learning. A Framework and a Method'. *Executive Development*, 7, 6, 29–32.

Chapter 2

Choosing effective teaching practices

> *Why* do you consider this, precisely this, right?
>
> (Nietzsche, 1882: 4, 335)

INTRODUCTION

How do you start your own lectures? Perhaps you dive straight in to make your first point, or maybe you begin with a statement of the learning outcomes the students will have achieved by the end of the session. Which of these approaches is more effective?

This chapter is designed to help you to develop the rational basis for your teaching, and thus to improve the way in which you choose between different teaching practices. We outline a number of progressively more rigorous ways to develop the rational basis of your teaching, starting with a look at your own experience of what practices are effective. The limitations of relying on your own instincts then lead us to see what you can learn from colleagues, and we conclude with the contribution of evaluation and research. At the same time we will also cover the relative merits of 'just getting on with the lecture', as opposed to 'bothering with learning outcomes'.

One thing, however, is clear – the evidence for any preferred practice will not just fall into your lap. The chapter also looks at realistic strategies to access the information that you require, as well as highlighting triggers that will prompt you to find evidence. After all, there are so many variables at play in education that one's personal context is highly relevant to how you teach. We do assume that you have at least some scope to determine which teaching practices you will employ. You may not have the freedom to choose whether to see students individually or in a large group, but you would usually have the scope to choose how to start a lecture.

EVIDENCE FROM YOUR OWN EXPERIENCE

What does your experience indicate is effective? You will have a store of your own memories as a student and as a teacher on which to draw. Perhaps you once tried to start a lecture by reading out a list of learning outcomes – and found a sea of bemused faces. You will have seen things that work and you will have noticed practices you want to avoid.

How good, though, is the evidence that stems from this experience? Perhaps you recited the list of outcomes while the students were half asleep, or preoccupied with an examination. The clear lesson is that you may well need to explore why something works or does not work. Unless you articulate and analyse the implications of your experience it may well be difficult to ascertain whether it is evidence or prejudice, an issue we shall explore further in Chapter 4.

What kinds of reasons do teachers propose to justify their practice? Table 2.1 summarises a range of reasons. Consider a particular teaching practice that you employ and see how many of these reasons in the table apply.

In many respects it is easy to make a case for the way that you teach; you simply select several reasons that appeal to you or support what you want to do. If you take a look at the individual entry route to become a registered practitioner of the Higher Education Academy in the UK (see www.heacademy.ac.uk), it is interesting to note that you could adopt this approach; but to what extent is such a case really rational? Why have you neglected so many other factors? Why have you accorded such weight to these particular reasons? Is it really the case that each of your reasons actually applies? Without explicitly addressing these concerns it would be rash to say that you had created a more genuine rational justification for adopting any particular practice. Nietzsche, certainly, was aware that our claims to rationality often simply reflect our own subjective choices rather than anything more objective.

Consider, for instance, the edited extract below from an assignment on a course in learning and teaching. The lecturer is seeking to justify her particular use of lectures that involve interaction with students. She cites her own experience, both as a student and lecturer, as evidence

TABLE 2.1 Possible reasons for adopting a teaching practice

Category	Reasons for adopting a practice
Personal	• This has worked for me in the past • I am interested in taking this on • I'm comfortable teaching in this fashion • I found it helpful when I was a student • This aligns with my personal approach to teaching
Student	• Students say that they like it this way • Students learn effectively and receive good grades • Students were able to complete the required tasks • I am able to address a wide range of learning outcomes • I receive positive feedback from the students • This leads to good relationships with the students • The students get involved and ask perceptive questions • Students choose my question on the examination above other questions
Professional	• The resources (technology, technicians, materials, etc.) are in place • I have time for this approach • This fits with the pattern of teaching in my department/ discipline • I am allowed to do this • The process is efficient • Colleagues tell me they like it

for the proposed practices, and proposes that involvement in one's own learning is important if one is to develop higher level skills. She considers one strategy that she might have employed and dismisses this.

There are a number of issues that would need to be addressed if we were to improve the rational basis for the practice she describes. Perhaps there are other strategies she could have considered which would not have involved forcing students to contribute:

- Introduce some individual exercises to prepare the students for the group or pair activities.

Box 2.1
JUSTIFICATION OF A LECTURER'S PRACTICE

It has not been long since I was a student myself. Therefore I have some insight into how students feel about long lectures in which the lecturer talks and they have to listen for the whole time. I will ensure my lectures are interactive, by using case studies and class exercises to generate interesting discussions. This will allow the students to learn through being involved rather than just by listening. As a result the student will develop critical thinking skills, a key outcome for the knowledge economy. Moreover a prerequisite of admission onto the programme is that students have a minimum of two years' work experience. They will thus have real world examples of the issues, making their input useful.

However, from past experience I know that this is easier said than done. In previous lectures I have given it has been very difficult to get some students to participate. Although I have used class exercises, group work and working in pairs, it has been difficult to get all students to participate without starting to embarrass them by calling out their names, a technique I was not willing to use. Therefore, what usually happens is that some students participate while others do not. This can be attributed to cultural reasons, in that some of my students may come from cultures that view the lecture as a 'teaching' venue in which the learner should not participate. This is difficult to change in a few weeks.

- Discuss some of the cultural issues openly with the students (although she does recognise the practical difficulties of shifting cultural expectations in a short space of time).
- Draw directly on the work experience that each student has undergone, and use this as a basis for encouraging students to contribute.

Does she effectively accept a teaching situation in which only some students will be able to attain these higher levels skills? She might also have argued that even in such situations where not all students directly contributed, they could still all attain the higher level skills as a result of the richer environment. Perhaps she could have ensured explicitly that the different contributions highlighted different viewpoints, emphasising the need for criticality. This would require an appreciation that more is required than simple 'involvement' for students to learn, even if this is seen as important.

In providing a more robust justification for your approach, you may find that certain aspects of the given practice are not as carefully thought out as you had imagined initially, and perhaps this will lead you to adapt the practice somewhat. An analysis of your own attempt to recite a list of learning outcomes might lead you to realise that a distracted student could easily miss out. This might lead you to put the outcomes onto a PowerPoint slide or overhead and to leave it up for a few seconds. (Such practices, of course, might be a more rational approach in light of your experience, but we have yet to see if they are effective!) Review point 2.1 below encourages you to put one of your own teaching practices under the microscope.

Review point 2.1
RATIONALE FOR PRACTICE

1 Select any practice that you carry out in your teaching and write half a page on why you carry out the practice in the way that you do (or select a short piece of writing where you have already provided a rationale for some aspect of your teaching).

2 Strengthen your rationale in the following ways:
- Underline each reason that you have advanced for employing the practice.
- Provide additional statements to support each reason.
- Provide further reasons to support your practice (looking at Table 2.1 may help to generate ideas for further reasons).
- Identify any reasons why you might not employ the practice, and provide a counter-argument to discount each reason.

You might also want to construct a case for adopting an alternative practice, perhaps one you have heard exists but of which you have no direct experience. It is, however, more difficult to construct a case for a method of teaching that you have little experience of using, or for which you have little interest. How do you even find out what the alternatives actually are? It is unrealistic to expect you to invent practical alternatives on the spot. Reasons for adopting something different may simply not occur to you. It is easy to dismiss any reasons that do come to mind. Only when you can realistically see what the alternatives actually involve are you in a position to begin to see which practice is likely to be more effective. Yet, although it may well be that another practice would be far better for you, your students and your context, you may have no experience of this, and so fail to weigh it up. If we are to determine the best way to start a lecture, we will need a thorough understanding of the competing options, and we will evidently need to go beyond our own immediate experience.

A further factor is also relevant: the context in which we teach is changing rapidly. The student body is no longer the elite group that it used to be, and the constraints of the growing market in higher education are beginning to be felt. The professional context in which you work can also shift overnight, with a reorganisation from departments into schools or a new policy initiative, say, on transferable skills. Even your own interests may change. The result is that the teaching practices you employ need revisiting on a regular basis. You thus need more than the ability to provide an argument for a certain way of teaching.

You could, of course, experiment and try out something new for yourself; but this is easier said than done. If you genuinely want to understand a new practice, it is hard to beat searching out alternatives and possible rationales for employing them. Any argument for a particular teaching practice does need to consider the alternatives; colleagues provide the first port of call.

DRAWING IDEAS FROM OTHERS

Engagement with colleagues from your own department, discipline and beyond enables you to access a wider range of experience. A conversation over coffee offers some scope to discuss alternative approaches to teaching – if someone in a very similar situation to yourself has tried something and found that it proved to be effective in their practice, it may be relatively easy for you to try it out for yourself. Perhaps a colleague has found that it works really well to start a lecture with a captivating anecdote that follows on from the last lecture – some disciplines lend themselves well to this type of approach. Another colleague may begin by addressing a question that they raised at the end of the last session, asking if any students are able to shed light on it.

However, conversations around teaching do not appear out of thin air. Someone needs to start them. Why not you? Share a problem or a success with a colleague who is interested in their teaching. The first time that you teach something, discuss how it went with a colleague afterwards, and see how he or she would have tackled the session or any problems that arose. You may, of course, receive a reaction such as 'If you start showing videos/using PowerPoint/inviting interaction, the students will expect it from everyone – so don't rock the boat'. In time you will learn who to talk to and who to avoid.

It helps if there are structured opportunities to discuss your teaching with colleagues. Seminars and workshops on teaching are relevant, as are mentoring relationships, organised discussions on courses in learning and teaching and so on. Team teaching offers particular possibilities, as we shall explore further in Chapter 6, especially where it involves working with experienced colleagues, although this is more likely to be a possibility in some disciplines than others. In Case study 2.1 Martyn Stewart describes the impact on his teaching that came from teaching with colleagues. Ideas can even transfer from one aspect of teaching to another: his experience, for instance, might encourage you to begin a lecture the way that you mean to go on, by ensuring that the students are actively involved. One advantage of such professional interactions is that there is usually scope to address the issue of why a practice might be effective in any given context. Your colleague might have indicated that they want their students to become actively involved in any lecture that they give – but that this only works in their experience if the students become interested in the material. Hence their immediate concern is to engage the interest of the students before encouraging student participation; and so perhaps they always begin classes with a compelling problem.

Case study 2.1
TEAM TEACHING

Fieldwork is a highly compact learning environment – effectively a module-worth of teaching and learning in a week – and this compactness is ideal for unpicking what works well in terms of timing and sequencing of learning activities. This case study describes how one particular trip had a marked impact in my understanding of what constituted effective teaching.

The majority of field trips centre around field lectures interspersed with part-day activities where students practise skills at new sites each day. This usually works well. However, in earth sciences, learning how to construct a geological map is quite a challenging task, requiring an understanding of landscape, rock identification and building a three-dimensional model of the underground strata.

One particular mapping trip I attended (as a teaching assistant) was structured quite differently. Instead of moving from site to site, the trip consisted of ten days based at the same location, which had a complex range of geological features. Early days of the trip consisted of no more than an hour of lecture to introduce new skills, but from then on and for the bulk of the ten days students were simply let go to work in teams to build up the map for themselves, with staff wandering around to provide guidance and feedback. The students certainly struggled during the early stages, but they were aware they had the luxury of time to develop their understandings and go through the process of discovering things for themselves rather than just 'wait for the lecturers to explain what's going on'.

Initially I considered this trip lacking in structure, scope and variety compared to previously attended trips planned as teacher-led mapping 'tours'. The key turning point here was the realisation that *this* was what mapping is actually like. It is not easy, it takes time and one has to develop these skills over time by getting immersed in the task. Cramming in as many sites as possible does not matter. And it worked – the quality of the students' work was extremely high, as was their confidence in their mapping capabilities as they advanced on to their field-based research projects.

This for me was the point at which I began to reflect on what the term 'student-centred learning' *really* meant – recognising the importance of letting go and especially creating space in any programme to enable enquiry-driven learning – I recall myself learning to map properly on independent fieldwork, rather than from listening to my teachers. It also sparked my understanding of appropriately aligning learning activities to intended learning outcomes. The skills to build a geological map are, by nature, exploratory and constructive. Therefore the activity has to be structured to allow the student to experience this. The legacy of this is that I now put great effort and thought into how I design new learning activities, and how the students engage with their learning, rather than 'what I shall teach'.

Martyn Stewart, Learning Development Unit and School of Biological and Earth Science, Liverpool John Moores University

Discussions with colleagues open up a wide range of experience to you, and yet further practice is articulated in written form. Case studies, practical texts on a given area of teaching and so on typically provide descriptions of practice and may give a rationale as to why the practices are appropriate. For instance, the case study 'Learning from objectives' (Yeo, 2001) describes a situation where the students on a lecture course on legal studies had become confused as to what should they focus their learning on, as the course was trying to cover too much. The lecturer responded by refocusing on the learning outcomes (referred to as learning objectives); cutting out material that was less important, distributing handouts that informed the students of the outcomes of each particular lecture, along with an outline of the lecture. This enabled the students to realise that the lecturer wanted them to appreciate a number of different approaches to criminal law, rather than simply to adopt a single method.

The written word, however, does not impose itself upon you in quite the way that your own colleagues or students are able to; the initiative has to rest with you. So why would you bother digging out a case study? Perhaps it is a requirement of a programme in learning and teaching that you are on, such as a Postgraduate Certificate in Learning and Teaching in Higher Education or a course for graduate teaching assistants; or maybe you have a problem in your teaching that you would like to address. You might be introducing a development into your teaching and are keen to avoid reinventing the wheel.

The range of descriptions of practice that are now available is increasingly rapidly, so the chances are that a relatively brief search will yield something interesting: to locate a relevant case study you might browse the websites indicated in Table 2.2; for practical texts on teaching and learning, see Table 2.3. It is worth remembering, though, that if the material is more remote from your own context, in the nature of the students, discipline, institution or so on, then more adaptation will be required if you are to adopt the process.

Some descriptions of practice incorporate or rely on formal evaluation – and it is here that we begin to move to a deeper level of rigour in our search for what works in higher education. Your own experience, contributions from colleagues and descriptions of practice are all at a relatively informal level. It is hard to tell if one practice genuinely results in an improvement over another practice. Evaluation is important because it helps to provide a more considered understanding as to why the practice was effective. For instance, in the case study from Yeo

TABLE 2.2 Online collections of case study and teaching materials, accessed 12 August 2005

Description of collection	Location
Resources from the Higher Education Academy	See under projects at www.connect.ac.uk; see also www.heacademy.ac.uk/resources.asp
Subject-specific resources from the Subject Centres of the Higher Education Academy	See under subject network at www.heacademy.ac.uk
General resources for learning and teaching	www.londonmet.ac.uk/deliberations/
The UK's emerging national collection of resources for learning and teaching	www.jorum.ac.uk
An international collection of resources	www.merlot.org/Home.po
Social Science Information Gateway	See under higher education at www.sosig.ac.uk

(2001), evaluation indicated that the changes made a significant difference to the student experience on the course, as the students' concerns had been addressed more directly. As people develop more systematic and comprehensive understanding of why a teaching practice is effective, we soon begin to touch on educational theory.

EVIDENCE FROM THEORY

Educational theory is notorious among staff in higher education for its jargon and apparent lack of relevance. Before dismissing the contribution of theory, perhaps it is worth putting the matter to the test.

In general, theory provides a framework within which to understand practice, and thus to justify the use of specific practices. We move beyond piling up a number of reasons to justify a practice to a situation in which each aspect of the practice can be explicitly justified with reference to an entire framework. We can see in Case study 2.2 (later in this section) that Anna Hiley specifically links the way she has constructed her teaching in light of the theory of deep and surface approaches to learning, helping to ensure that it more directly matches the needs of her students.

TABLE 2.3 Practical literature on learning and teaching

Focus of practice	Suggested text(s)
General	*A Handbook for Learning and Teaching in Higher Education* (Fry *et al.*, 2003)
	The Lecturer's Toolkit (Race, 2004)
	The 'Key Guides for Effective Teaching in Higher Education' series (from RoutledgeFalmer)
	Teaching for Quality Learning at University (Biggs, 2003)
	Rethinking University Teaching (Laurillard, 2002)
Teaching and supporting learning	*Giving a Lecture* (Dennick and Exley, 2004a)
	Small Group Teaching (Dennick and Exley, 2004b)
	Using C&IT to Support Teaching (Chin, 2004)
	Learning in Groups (Jaques, 2000)
Course design	*Designing Courses for Higher Education* (Toohey, 1999)
	The Challenge of Problem Based Learning (Boud and Feletti, 1998)
Assessment	*Assessing Students' Written Work* (Haines, 2004)
	Assessment Matters in Higher Education (Brown and Glasner, 1999)
Student support	*A Handbook for Personal Tutors* (Wheeler and Birtle, 1993)
Subject-specific literature	Supporting New Academic Staff database: www.heacademy.ac.uk/snasdatabase.asp
	'Effective Learning and Teaching in Higher Education' series (from RoutledgeFalmer)

Theory is particularly useful when trying out a practice for the first time, or introducing a genuine innovation – we need not proceed simply on the basis of trial and error. Of course, some theories are more powerful and far reaching than other theories, providing a sound basis for a wider range of innovations. Some of the more common theories of learning are given in Table 2.4, with Jarvis (2002) providing a good introduction.

TABLE 2.4 Established theories of learning

Theory	Description
Deep and surface approaches to learning	The way in which a student approaches the tasks they carry out helps to determine the effectiveness of their learning. A deep approach is characterised by a search for both meaning and links between ideas. A surface approach concentrates simply on getting the task done, or on rote learning.
Experiential learning	This broad theoretical perspective recognises that learning involves far more than simply mastering a given body of knowledge. The experience that learners bring with them or engage in on a course can motivate and shape learning.
Constructivism	Emphasis is placed on the way in which learning involves the student creating concepts or constructs, as a result of processes that are personal to the learner. Cognitive processes, for instance, will involve the learner's direction of their own thinking. Some theories place a particular emphasis on the role that social interaction plays in the construction of understanding.
Behaviourism	Here the focus is on behavioural outcomes of learning, so that in effect a response can be measured to a stimulus. This might involve substantial repetition to establish the response (rote learning), but equally, more open processes of discovery are possible. In both cases, however, outcomes are established at the outset.

Theory also enables you to diagnose why certain problems have occurred or suggest improvements. The theory of learning styles is one of the more accessible theories within higher education. Learners are, for instance, classed as visual, written, auditory or practical. This might suggest that simply reading out a list of learning outcomes would then appeal only to a limited number of your students: those with a preference for learning in an auditory style. Our theoretical perspective would suggest that it might be worth presenting the list on a PowerPoint slide, but also linking an activity to the outcomes or expanding your introduction with a visual image or images.

Case study 2.2 DRAWING ON THEORY

In industry, engineers are valued for their ability to exercise judgement within a practical context. This involves implicit knowledge, and is indeterminate, intuitive and can involve lateral thinking. In my experience, however, students usually come to university thinking that the study of engineering involves memorising information and repeating it within an examination. To support the transition to higher education, I wanted to create a first-year module that promoted investigative, analytical and creative skills for identifying and solving problems.

I was aware that a well-established theory had already identified these different patterns of learning – the theory of approaches to learning. Students who take a deep approach are actively involved in choosing how to focus their learning, making connections between different ideas. By contrast, students who follow a surface approach have no intention of actually understanding what is going on; their aim is, rather, to be able to reproduce what they have learnt. For me the question became: how can I encourage a deep approach to learning on my module?

I took the design process as my starting point, as this is a fundamental activity for construction engineers. For me design is the process of investigating a problem in a critical way to define an optimum solution, given a particular context. Rather than tell the students about the design process, which I was convinced would produce a surface approach, I wanted the students to make sense of the process by actually carrying out its different stages. Therefore, I introduced seven two-hour workshops that focused separately on different aspects of the process, and on related factors. Breaking up the process into several stages was an essential factor in this as it helped them to make the necessary connections between the different stages; teamwork also supported the students in together making these connections. Otherwise they could easily have been swamped with the complexity of the process. The theory of approaches to learning thus assisted me in shaping the methods I used to teach the students.

Anna Hiley, School of Mechanical, Aerospace and Civil Engineering, University of Manchester

You may wish to revisit your earlier rationale from Review point 2.1 above in light of a specific theory, perhaps one from Table 2.4, and then rework your rationale in light of this theory. Alternatively, if you are about to plan your teaching for the next semester or are about to design a course unit, you may wish to consider doing so in light of a specific theory. An assignment on a programme in learning and teaching that requires you to analyse or justify your practice would also provide a suitable opportunity to test the relevance of a specific theory to your practice. Unless you actually work with a theory in the context of your practice, you are unlikely to be able to test the effectiveness of the theory.

EVIDENCE FROM RESEARCH

There is a further stage in engaging with theory – and that is directly to access research studies or reviews of research rather than rely on presentations of theory from others. The advantage is that you may be able to find specific studies that are directly relevant to your work. Clearly this involves additional time – but the extra effort may be worthwhile when developing initial expertise, designing a new course or spearheading an innovation.

We outline here an explicit approach to reviewing the research on teaching practices, developed by one of us along with a colleague (Kahn and Macdonald, 2005). The process builds on ideas from evidence-based medicine and from systematic reviews of research. The aim in this is to go beyond randomly picking out a few vaguely relevant studies. Following a more systematic process is likely to yield a more rational basis for your teaching; ideally this will be carried out in collaboration with colleagues,

Determine the aim of the review

What do you hope to achieve by your review?

Outline the underpinning practice and theory

What theoretical concepts underpin this area of practice?

Set the review question

Decide on an answerable question that addresses the effectiveness of the practice(s) in question.

Locate the best evidence

Select the information resources to search –Informal channels: Google Scholar web search or recommendations from colleagues. Formal channels: hand search a relevant journal, such as *Teaching in Higher Education or Studies in Higher Education*; British Education Index, and the associated databases from the USA and Australia; Educational Research Abstracts Online; and other databases available from www.sosig.ac.uk/education/.

Choose keywords to form the initial basis for the search (drawing on the review question and the underpinning theory).

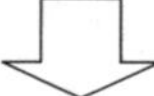

Critically appraise the studies that you locate

¥ How relevant is the study to your review question?
¥ Does the study outline justify the methodology employed?
¥ What does the research conclude about the effectiveness of the practice?
¥ What does the research have to say about why the practice is effective?
¥ What systemic patterns are evident across all of the studies

Apply the evidence in practice

How can I adapt my own practice in light of the evidence?

FIGURE 2.1 Flow chart indicating a process for reviewing the research on a specific aspect of learning and teaching

with each person responsible for an element of the review, as the richness of the interactions will improve the outcome. The full process is outlined in Figure 2.1, although it is quite possible that even a limited search of the relevant literature will lead to a useful study.

In our case, a search within the British Educational Index with the words 'learning outcomes' yielded two studies in particular. Hussey and Smith (2002) claim that:

> Learning outcomes have value when properly conceived and used in ways that respect their limitations and exploit their virtues, but they are damaging to education if seen as precise prescriptions that must be spelled out in detail before teaching can begin and which are objective and measurable devices suitable for monitoring educational practices.
>
> (p. 222)

Hussey and Smith (2003), meanwhile, go on to argue that teaching requires a careful balance between a lecturer's intentions for student learning and the contributions that students themselves make; and that being too upfront about the outcomes of an individual session could upset that balance. While these two articles are not backed-up substantive research studies and rely instead on arguing their case, they still provide a real caution to the way in which we employ learning outcomes when actually teaching students.

Review point 2.2
A COMPARISON

1 Construct a rationale for an alternative practice to the one that you described above on page 14. You should incorporate reasons from at least three of the following sources into your rationale: your own experience; colleagues; practical literature; theoretical literature; research studies.

2 Which rationale do you find more convincing? The rationale created during the earlier review point, or the rationale for this activity?

CONCLUSION: BEYOND WHAT IS RATIONAL

So, what is the best way to start a lecture? We have begun to see that the issues relate quite directly to issues such as the way in which students learn, to the relationship between students and tutor, and to the motivation that students bring with them. As with many educational questions, we have been unable to provide a fully unambiguous answer, but at least we have gone far beyond a casual aside about inattentive students!

At this point it makes sense to return to your own earlier attempt to create a basis for a specific teaching practice. Can you now construct a compelling case to adopt a different practice? You might like to apply the protocol to the practice that you selected for Review point 2.1 and to what you consider the leading alternative. In any case, together with the further insights that can be yielded from colleagues, descriptions of practice, theory and research studies, we are now in a position to create a more rational basis for our practice.

The case that you create for an alternative practice might well be more compelling than your original practice, but there is still no guarantee that you will actually adopt the 'better' alternative. When it comes down to it, tomorrow morning you might still do nothing more than read out your list of learning outcomes. One might say that the choices we make about teaching are determined on more than rational grounds, as we have already begun to appreciate.

As we shall see in the next chapter, much more is required than an analysis of competing practices. After all, the predictive power of even the best educational theory remains relatively weak – given the huge range of circumstances, context, culture and discipline that affect educational outcomes – certainly when compared to the natural sciences. Counter examples will always abound. The effectiveness of a practice thus cannot easily be considered in isolation from one's own context and approach to teaching. Someone who is simply used to presenting material in a session rather than also interacting with the students is likely to find it more difficult to adopt an approach that requires interaction.

Furthermore, we will see that this is only the beginning of the matter – every chapter in the book contributes further insights into how to teach more effectively. Professional life does provide a range of natural opportunities to develop a broad base of evidence for your teaching, but we still have to take the opportunities. Developing your teaching still requires a willingness to invest yourself in the process.

REFERENCES

Biggs, J. (2003) *Teaching for Quality Learning at University*, second edition. Buckingham: Society for Research into Higher Education and Open University Press.

Boud, D. and Feletti, G. (eds) (1998) *The Challenge of Problem Based Learning*, second edition. London: Kogan Page.

Brown, S. and Glasner, A. (eds) (1999) *Assessment Matters in Higher Education: Choosing and Using Diverse Approaches*. Buckingham: Society for Research into Higher Education and Open University Press.

Chin, P. (2004) *Using C&IT to Support Teaching*. London: RoutledgeFalmer.

Dennick, R. and Exley, K. (2004a) *Giving a Lecture*. London: RoutledgeFalmer.

Dennick, R. and Exley, K. (2004b) *Small Group Teaching*. London: Routledge Falmer.

Fry, H., Ketteridge, S. and Marshall, S. (eds) (2003) *A Handbook for Teaching and Learning in Higher Education*, second edition. London: Kogan Page.

Haines, C. (2004) *Assessing Students' Written Work*. London: RoutledgeFalmer.

Hussey, T. and Smith, P. (2002) 'The Trouble with Learning Outcomes'. *Active Learning in Higher Education*, 3, 3, 220–33.

____ and ____ (2003) 'The Uses of Learning Outcomes'. *Teaching in Higher Education*, 8, 3, 357–68.

Jaques, D. (2000) *Learning in Groups*, third edition. London: Kogan Page.

Jarvis, P., Holford, J. and Griffin, C. (2002) *The Theory and Practice of Learning*. London: Kogan Page.

Kahn, P. E. and MacDonald, R. (2005) 'A Systematic Approach for Staff and Educational Developers Who Would Like Evidence to Inform their Practice'. *Educational Developments*, 6, 2, 17–20.

Laurillard, D. (2002) *Rethinking University Teaching: A Conversational Framework for the Effective Use of Learning Technologies*, second edition. London: RoutledgeFalmer.

Nietzsche, F. (1882) *The Gay Science*, translated by Walter Kaufmann, New York, Vintage Books, 1974.

Race, P. (2004) *The Lecturer's Toolkit: A Practical Guide to Learning, Teaching and Assessment*, second edition. London: RoutledgeFalmer.

Toohey, S. (1999) *Designing Courses for Higher Education*. Buckingham: Society for Research into Higher Education and Open University Press.

Wheeler, S. and Birtle, J. (1993) *A Handbook for Personal Tutors*. Buckingham: Society for Research into Higher Education and Open University Press.

Yeo, S. (2001) 'Learning from Objectives', in Edwards, H., Smith, B. and Webb, G. *Lecturing: Case Studies, Experience and Practice*. London: Kogan Page.

FURTHER READING

Jarvis, P. (ed.) (2001) *The Theory and Practice of Teaching*. London: Kogan Page.

Chapter 3

Inspiration for teaching

> Teachers must be better compensated, freed from bureaucratic harassment, given a role in academic governance, and provided with the best possible methods and materials. But none of that will transform education if we fail to cherish – and challenge – the human heart that is the source of good teaching.
>
> (Parker Palmer, 1998: 3)

INTRODUCTION

What is compelling or inspiring in human experience? Great art has the capacity to attract us, and to take us beyond ourselves. Rachmaninov's Second Piano Concerto and Michaelangelo's *Last Judgement* hold our attention. We see a similar effect in political rhetoric, where sound bites and spin are designed to sway voters, and in the addictive power of computer games. We are taken beyond our immediate reality to the promise of a better life or to another world.

The rousing lecture, meanwhile, is an archetypal image of inspiration, to which listeners respond with heartfelt dedication to learning; but our lectures can just as easily send students to sleep. Heavy workloads, limited time with any individual student, bureaucracy and greater rewards for research: all these can only too easily quash our enjoyment in teaching, and make it much less likely that we will hold our students' attention.

How then is it possible to make our teaching more compelling, both for students and tutor? This is the question that we explore in this chapter. We focus first of all on the subject itself: after all, many lecturers teach because their discipline fascinates them. Teaching also involves a connection with students. It is often the enthusiasm of the teacher that makes the difference for the student. It does, though, take something to sustain this connection with your students: the tutor also needs to draw on the support of colleagues and on his or her own inner reserves. We will see that it is these sources, rather than the ability to perform in front of a group of students, that makes the difference.

CONNECTING WITH YOUR SUBJECT

How did you come to enjoy your subject? Perhaps flashes of insight first hooked you, as concepts and theories came alive. Research then allowed you to open up new ideas for yourself. This suggests that a process of discovery is at the heart of any engagement with a subject. The way in which we teach, however, may not actually reflect our own pattern of learning, as Bill Hutchings describes in Case study 3.1 later in this section. He realised that the subject itself should colour the way in which it is taught, an issue that Rowland (2000) explores. Rowland notes, for instance:

> A teacher of design who did not encourage students to be inventive in their learning would be failing to teach students to become designers. And in Philosophy, for example, Plato describes Socrates as an exponent of a particular philosophical method, but this Socratic form of question and answer is also a pedagogic practice.
>
> (p. 113)

A body of research has now grown up around these issues more widely, as to how lecturers conceive their teaching: a recent review identifies two broad categories, as evident in Table 3.1.

When adopting an information-focused approach, the tutor primarily seeks to impart knowledge to the student. The tutor's concerns, for instance, may be centred on developing a good set of lecture notes, or on how best to organise the material for the students. By contrast, a focus on the process of learning requires the students to take a more active role. Students are more likely to make their own connections between findings, and thus to experience the discipline as more compelling. This approach is also easier to sustain in the long run, as more depends on the students, and less time needs to be spent preparing materials.

TABLE 3.1 Broad conceptions of teaching

Conception of teaching	Description
Information-focused	The tutor believes that it is important to tell the students what they need to know, structuring the information for them.
Process-focused	The tutor sees their role as creating an environment in which the students can learn. This may involve both developing an effective relationship with your students and challenging their preconceptions of your subject.

Source: after Kember, 1997.

Case study 3.1
BLAH BLAH BLAH

It was June 1998 that it happened. I had completed what I thought had been a pretty successful teaching year. My second-year undergraduate groups had responded well to their introduction to eighteenth-century literature, a recondite area even to quite advanced students. My third-year groups had contributed fully to the seminars, and had all achieved excellent degrees. Even the poetry of Alexander Pope – our greatest English poet when properly understood, our most boring English poet when not – had seemed to evoke positive responses.

As I basked in the sun of complacency, one of my best third-year students came to thank me for the course, for the materials I had provided and for the helpful teaching. We had a chat about her future plans and her career aims, all of which had been carefully thought through. As we said goodbye until graduation day, she cheerfully added, 'At least now I don't have to read any more poems.' Well, there we were. The sum total of my achievement that year: an excellent student, happy with her degree, kind enough to take the trouble to come and see me (and to leave me a thank-you card), now going out into the community with this message for the future of literature: 'At least I don't have to read any more poems.' I toyed with the possibility that she had been displaying characteristically English irony. Had there been a twinkle in her eye as she spoke? But, no; she had been, I was sure, entirely serious.

I looked back at the learning outcomes for my course. There they all were: a detailed knowledge of the works of . . ., deployment of skills of critical and analytical thinking and research at a level appropriate to blah blah . . . skills of written expression blah blah. And, yes, these important outcomes had been achieved, and, yes, my excellent student had well deserved her excellent degree, and I had no reason but to feel satisfied that I had carried out my professional duties. But I went home depressed.

I woke to the realisation that, amidst all the (quality assured) learning outcomes I had so carefully plotted and realised, there were some missing. And these were the very ones that had drawn me to the teaching profession in the first place: the excitement of discovery; the delight in understanding; the intellectual achievement of close and detailed reading; the intensity of discussion and debate; the power of art to open far other worlds and other seas; the chance to communicate all these to sensitive and intelligent people – in sum, the purpose of reading, this was missing.

'The only end of writing is to enable the readers better to enjoy life, or better to endure it,' wrote Samuel Johnson in a work that figured largely on the course I had taught. I decided at that point that, whatever else I did, I would try to make my teaching – and the students' learning – consistent with what the authors I was teaching had to say, and with what, ultimately, I felt the subject to be about. And so I looked for learning methods aligned with the basic principles of the subject and . . .

Bill Hutchings, School of Arts, Histories and Cultures, University of Manchester

Paying attention to the process of learning helps to expose students to the patterns of thinking and investigating within their discipline. When higher education was the preserve of an elite, students might have been expected to discover and master these inner workings for themselves, but with high student–staff ratios this is too much to expect. In this approach, every problem, issue or theory provides an opportunity explicitly to illustrate something of the internal logic of the discipline: Palmer (1998: 120) calls this teaching from the microcosm. Box 3.1 provides an example from mathematics. This approach enables the tutor to expose the patterns of thought that the students need to grasp if they are to make sense of the discipline, and its ideas and problems.

Kember's review (1997) indicates that tutors who adopt the process-focused approach are significantly more effective in supporting learning than those adopting the information-focused approach. The research, however, also indicates that it is difficult for a lecturer to shift from one conception to another, and that even when one professes to hold a certain conception of teaching, one's actual practice may reflect a

Box 3.1
TEACHING FROM THE MICROCOSM

As many readers will know from bitter experience of learning mathematics, if you have failed to understand an initial concept, it will be almost impossible to make sense of a more advanced concept that builds on it. For instance, in order to understand the concept of 'addition' – how to add one number to another – you need first to understand the idea of a 'number'. However, students cannot rely on the tutor always to identify the problem for them. They need to be able to take a look at an advanced concept and identify all of the concepts that contribute to it, so that they can then make sure they understand all of these more basic concepts, as one of us has explored in a study guide for students (Kahn, 2001).

If the tutor only ever presents the students with an ordered presentation of material, today's typical student is unlikely ever to learn this skill. Effective teaching of mathematics will thus use specific examples to highlight this for students, and provide opportunities for them to develop it.

different conception, an issue we will explore in Chapter 4 when we consider the difference between espoused theories and theories in action. It will clearly be difficult to retain any inspiration for teaching if this is the case. So it will be worth reviewing the techniques that you actually employ in your teaching.

Review point 3.1
ANALYSING YOUR TEACHING

1 Pick out a number of techniques that you employ in your teaching, and identify how each technique fits with the descriptions given above in Table 3.1.

2 Identify some of the basic patterns of thinking that students need to master within your own discipline.

CONNECTING WITH YOUR STUDENTS

The photos are of delightful pupils. Smiles and laughter in their faces, with accompanying slogans that draw you in: 'Children are creative, energetic . . . always surprising'; 'Work with the most exciting people in the country'; 'Linguists. Would you like to learn new words?' How can any other career be quite as enticing? The adverts are almost enough to convince you to go into school teaching.

Students in higher education may not be quite as young, but they are still full of creative energy; and by connecting more closely to your students, you stand to gain a source of inspiration for both your teaching and your research. The issue is how to achieve this result in a realistic and authentic fashion. Is this possible with 400 students in a lecture theatre, with whom you may feel you have little in common?

The obvious solution is to structure teaching in a way that promotes a dialogue with your students. Direct contact with students – what you might call the act of teaching – forms the basis for your relationship with them, so it makes sense to build a conversation into proceedings. A conversation is unlikely to result if the teacher only presents material. You can ask for questions at the end of the lecture, but there is no particular reason why the students need respond. Instead, you need to build the expectation, or even requirement, of a conversation into the structure of the teaching, as Laurillard (2001) argues. The way in which technology can support this conversation is an integral part of her argument, enabling students to describe their own understandings, facilitating feedback, building flexibility into tasks, encouraging review of work and so on. This dialogue with students allows significant scope for variety in the classroom. How can you sustain passion for something when it always runs exactly as you have planned, and where there is no element of surprise?

Teaching that incorporates dialogue also sets the overall tone for your relationships with the students. You have a real basis for taking an interest in them, both within and beyond the immediate teaching situation. Graduate teaching assistants clearly have an advantage in getting to know their students, as the inhibitions on both sides are likely to be lower, but so do tutors with modest class sizes. Personal knowledge of every student is particularly helpful in small-group work, where it is certainly easier when you know which student is likely to respond well to which question, or when you connect a point with a prior experience or strength of their own, but even in larger groups, knowledge of the interests of at least a few students will help you to build rapport with the class. Emotional intelligence has a role to play here. As Mortiboys (2002: 28) explains, 'being emotionally intelligent with your students necessitates *seeing* them as individuals even if you cannot pretend to *know* them as individuals'.

Review point 3.2
FOSTERING DIALOGUE

Pick out a number of techniques that you employ in your teaching, and identify how each one either promotes a dialogue with your students or closes it down.

So far it would seem possible to relate to students largely on the basis of technique – a carefully constructed dialogue that is supported by judicious interest in your students. This might result in you doing little more than just manipulating your students' thinking, even if in the pursuit of an agreed set of learning outcomes. But is this enough, for you and for them? Students would surely sense that you are remote from them. You also need to be willing to put yourself to at least a measure of trouble. If the whole teaching situation is so obviously designed to suit the teacher rather than the student, then the students will sense that you are not interested. When students make reasonable requests or genuine suggestions to improve the teaching environment, excuses are likely to follow in their wake.

Often, our inexperience as teachers can make us more pointed and barbed than we mean to be. We don protective armour in order to create a defence between 'us' and 'them'. Such a defence can take physical form, in the shape of desks and lecterns that create barriers between us and our students, establishing a gulf that is both mental and environmental. Or it can take on a pseudo-intellectual form, making us contemptuous or sneering in the face of apparently inane student questions. Before we know it, we have grown into the crusty, scowling, harrumphing lecturers that we despised, feared or resented when we were undergraduates. You are thinking 'That won't happen to me'? Maybe not, but in order to make it definitely not, let us think about the actions we need to take to become inspiring, authentic and genuine teachers.

We cannot avoid a more fundamental discussion of the place of values in teaching, and of the wider environment in which students learn. A positive learning environment that engenders feelings of respect, acceptance and trust is vitally important in establishing a positive dialogue, where tutors and students can build up relationships built on trust rather than on roles. Establishing a learning climate in this way supports and encourages questioning, critical thinking and ultimately deeper learning. As Jarvis notes (2001: 80), supporting students in realising their capacity for learning is the trademark of a good tutor that moves education 'from a delivery of static knowledge to a dialogical relationship where knowledge is co-created' – surely our ultimate aim.

In order to establish this environment, you need to be willing to expose something of yourself, even to risk something. Teaching from the microcosm facilitates this, allowing you to expose your own struggles to master the discipline. Some forms of teaching allow for risk-taking, in a way that giving a carefully crafted lecture may discourage. It is easy to fear that students will take advantage of this openness. John Cowan in Case study 3.2 illustrates that both the students and the tutor have a great deal to gain. John could have decided not to be open about his own attempt to reflect, perhaps fearing a loss of respect, but he was willing to take the risk. Occasionally a student might indeed take advantage of such trust, but to build a relationship on the basis of fear is hardly likely to create the kind of virtuous circle that trust engenders. Relying on trust means that the student is more likely to trust you with their own faltering attempts to understand your discipline.

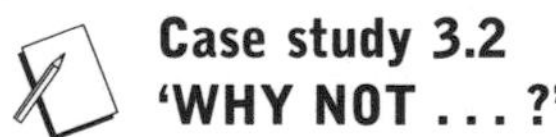

Case study 3.2
'WHY NOT . . . ?'

I was travelling on holiday to Italy with my wife, and had taken with me one of Jenny Moon's books on reflective learning journals, intending to re-read and look out for what I might have missed on my first (thorough) reading some time earlier. During a long delay in the departure lounge, I skimmed over mention of a teacher who had shared one of his reflective journals with his students. I thought, 'Maybe I should do that?' As I mused, my conscience troubled me. I recalled all I had read, and been told by my own students, of their sensitivity in putting private thoughts on paper, and having someone else comment thereon. I asked myself rhetorically, 'Why don't I ask of me what I ask of them?' And so, on my return to Britain, as I went into another semester of facilitating reflective process analyses, I set myself the same task, though in my own context, doing what I asked of the students, and passing my efforts on to them – for comment, if they so wished.

For four weeks this worked quite well. My journals exemplified the type of self-questioning we sought to promote, and the students were appreciative of seeing examples. Then I wrote a journal that was dreadful. I had almost deleted it from the hard disk, to start anew, when it occurred to me that the students would not have the luxury of enough time (or ideas) to produce a second journal if the first proved poor. So I just sent out the unsatisfactory journal, with a brief note explaining what I have reported here.

In the ten days that followed, I received a steady stream of comments to the effect that 'It's so good to see that a lecturer can make a mess of reflecting, too!' That strengthened my resolve to continue this practice, and to receive each journal submitted for comment with my usual acknowledgement, 'Thanks for your Journal 6, Eliz; I'll hope to be back with comments by tomorrow evening', to which I would now add, 'I'm attaching my own Journal 6, and will welcome any comments that *you* have, for *me*.'

This innovation radically changed the tutor/student relationship. Instead of my being a facilitator, we were peers, albeit senior and junior, sharing and able to mull over similar experiences. And all because I twice asked myself, 'Why not . . . ?'

John Cowan, formerly of the Social Sciences Course Team,
UHI Millennium Institute

Courage is required for anyone who wants to teach in an inspirational fashion. We can see a further link here with the care that a teacher offers to their students. MacIntyre (1981: 192, cited in Day, 2004: 30) observes that if I am unwilling to risk harm to myself I call into question the genuineness of my concern for someone. The nature of the care we extend to our students will differ from that given in schools, but it nonetheless remains an essential part of teaching.

We can think of further values that are important as well. Fairness to students is essential. Indeed, research on school teaching is clear that a passion for all pupils to succeed is a common factor in high-quality teachers (Hopkins and Stern, 1996). This does not mean that we always treat students in an identical fashion; any parent of more than one child can predict that this will not lead to fairness. At times we will need to take into account the needs and situation of each student. This provides one reason why it is indeed fair to provide additional support to students with disabilities. We can go on to list a whole range of qualities that the inspirational teacher needs to possess – patience, hope, dogged persistence and so on. The issue then is how we can develop such habits. It may be useful to begin by drawing up a list of principles that can become a personal 'code of conduct'. Here is an example of what might be included in such a list (adapted from Murray *et al.*, 1996):

- proficiency in subject knowledge
- expertise in learning, teaching and assessing
- support of student development
- respectful relationships with students
- consideration for confidentiality
- readiness to collaborate with colleagues
- recognition of institutional expectations.

Review point 3.3
A PERSONAL CODE

1 Consider the above list and how it relates to any conception you might have currently of a personal code of conduct.

2 Expand on each of the headings in order to begin to develop your own personal code.

If this remains a list, of course, then it will hardly serve its purpose. You will also need to review your own teaching in light of this code, adapting it as your career unfolds.

CONNECTING WITH YOUR COLLEAGUES

Teaching does not just involve a relationship between the tutor and the students. Any performance in front of a group of students is made possible by extensive work behind the scenes. Just as the act of teaching provides a basis for a dialogue with students, this backstage work provides a basis for relationships with colleagues.

We have already seen in the previous chapter that the capacity to develop your teaching is linked to the quality and range of the relationships you have with your colleagues. Ideas for new approaches to teaching frequently come from your colleagues. Equally, the support we receive from our colleagues can make a significant difference in our ability to cope with stress related to teaching. This is not surprising given that we are social animals: reality is a web of relationships. We thus need to find ways to connect with our colleagues.

One key strategy is to carry out some tasks in common, as Knight suggests (2002): professional development activity, curriculum reviews and the organisation of teaching are all relevant. It is clearly more difficult for teachers who work part-time to establish this connection with their colleagues: doctoral students with occasional teaching or visiting staff are often in a weak position. Opportunities may still arise for such staff, and the issue then is to decide whether the investment of your time is worthwhile. In some ways the temptation is to avoid any collaborative tasks related to teaching, or to engage only minimally, particularly if research is seen as a greater priority; but there is a cost to this approach.

Strong relationships with colleagues are important in the longer term, particularly in dealing with change:

- You may want to initiate a change in the way that you teach, one which has implications for your colleagues. You stand a greater chance of carrying the change if you can involve your colleagues in a constructive way, and this in turn depends on your relationships with them. One of us recently experienced a telling example in this regard, when a new programme proposal was strongly criticised by a committee: but what else might you expect if you have had no effective relationship with any member of the committee and none of them has contributed to the design! (However, as we shall see shortly, this was not the end of the matter.)
- Many ideas are killed in their early stages because colleagues have different priorities. Imagine trying to sustain inspiration for teaching when your ideas are instantly dismissed.
- Challenges arise when you find that teaching in your school or department is shifting in a direction you would rather not follow. In this case it may help to become involved and adapt what is going on, rather than looking on helplessly from the

sidelines, with all the attendant stress involved. Change is always easier to manage when you know the system from the inside.

The way in which you collaborate with colleagues is also relevant. Proceedings can operate on strictly task-based grounds – on getting things done. Alternatively it is possible to use the activity as a springboard for further discussion about issues in your teaching. Just as it was important to be open with students about your own struggles with the discipline, so openness with colleagues can lead to genuinely helpful discussions. Lack of interest may be a common response, but you can at least pick and choose the colleagues with whom you initiate discussion.

There are, of course, a variety of ways in which such discussion can lead. Moaning about students, or their earlier experiences at school, is one time-honoured approach, but this rarely helps you to develop your teaching. By contrast, research has recently highlighted the value of appreciation. Appreciative enquiry begins with an unconditional positive question that 'guides inquiry agendas and focuses attention towards the most life-giving, life-sustaining aspects of organisational existence' (Ludema *et al.*, 2001: 189). This contrasts with the relentless criticism that is often found in higher education. An enquiry begins with the choice of a focus, perhaps a powerful source of inspiration in your own teaching. The theory is that growth occurs where we focus our attention. Judgement is still present in the choice of where to focus attention, but whereas criticism can destroy dialogue, appreciation encourages further disclosure and creativity, fostering new relationships. Once you have explored a source of inspiration, a full appreciative enquiry would then involve finding ways to extend its reach: dreaming of new possibilities, designing and sustaining new initiatives, while drawing others into the cycle.

Review point 3.4
APPRECIATING YOUR TEACHING

Pick an area of your teaching that works well. Initiate a discussion with a colleague to explore why it works well.

YOUR OWN INNER WORLD

Where do you find it in yourself to take risks with your students, or to maintain a clear vision of your own direction as change occurs? Sooner or later we come to the inner reserves of the teacher, as Palmer stresses in *Courage to Teach* (1998). How do you develop and sustain these reserves? He argues that 'the most practical thing we can achieve in any kind of work is insight into what is happening inside us as we do it' (p. 5). Insight into what drives us is essential if we are to sustain and develop any commitment to teaching. The techniques of review that we consider in Chapter 4 will be particularly important in this, as you search for insight into what works for yourself.

This search needs to be realised in concrete ways. You may want to conduct a series of limited investigations into the forms of teaching that energise you, perhaps feeding a few ideas to colleagues for their response. This is certainly better than a vague attempt to 'find yourself'. Your attitudes to your students, subject and colleagues are all important, as are your beliefs about teaching or the emotions you experience while teaching. Indeed, you may have reacted to certain parts of this chapter because of these attitudes and beliefs; this could even provide the basis for discussion with colleagues.

As an example, we highlight one area here: self-efficacy, or the belief in your own capacity to make a difference (see, for instance, Dweck, 1999). The strength of such self-belief affects whether you will carry a task through to its end. The literature indicates that those with greater self-efficacy are more likely to persevere with complex activity that is not amenable to instant solutions – and developing your teaching undoubtedly falls into this category. The new programme proposal mentioned above that was dismissed by one committee was shortly afterwards accepted by another one. The chair was the same, but the rest of the committee were largely close colleagues and no other interests were at stake this time. Perseverance clearly makes a difference in the political world that constitutes higher education.

How, then, might an enquiry help you to understand and develop the role of self-belief in your teaching?

Review point 3.5
ONE STAGE FURTHER

1 Pick a development in your teaching, however small, that you are tempted to give up on, and take it one stage further, perhaps by adapting it once more.

2 Compare your experience with another situation in which you gave up relatively quickly.

In order to make a meaningful comparison, you will need to collect some data, not just a few hazy memories. Make detailed notes on each situation, following this with a commentary on each description that pulls out interesting features and common patterns. You could also take a look at the consequences for student learning of your decision to end the development or to persevere with it. A further stage would be to discuss some of the resulting issues with your colleagues, noting their responses. You will want to employ both inner and outer arcs of attention, as Marshall (2001) explores. Inner arcs focus on patterns, themes or ongoing dilemmas within your own thoughts, words or actions. Outer arcs focus on the issues you choose to raise with others. Insights into your self-belief will only result from such varied attention rather than wishful thinking.

CONCLUSION

Inspiration for teaching does not arise by chance: it requires a readiness to search, in whatever places you find most helpful. Perhaps you need to escape for a day each term to review your practice, a journal in which to record your thoughts, a colleague who is willing to chat to you once every couple of weeks, a text that provides a new perspective on your discipline so that it retains its freshness for you, or contact with young people outside the university setting. There are plenty of ways to find inspiration for teaching so that it compels both ourselves and our students.

REFERENCES

Day, C. (2004) *A Passion for Teaching*. London: RoutledgeFalmer.

Dweck, C. (1999) *Self Theories: Their Role in Motivation, Personality and Development*. Philadelphia, PA: Psychology Press.

Hopkins, D. and Stern, D. (1996) 'Quality Teachers, Quality Schools'. *Teaching and Teacher Education* 12, 5, 501–17.

Jarvis, P. (ed.) (2001) *The Theory and Practice of Teaching*. London: Kogan Page.

Kahn, P. E. (2001) *Studying Mathematics and Its Applications*. Basingstoke: Palgrave.

Kember, D. (1997) 'A Reconceptualisation of the Research into University Academics' Conceptions of Teaching'. *Learning and Instruction*, 7, 3, 255–75.

Knight, P. (2002) *Being a Teacher in Higher Education*. Buckingham: Society for Research into Higher Education/Open University Press.

Laurillard, D. (2001) *Rethinking University Teaching*, second edition. London: RoutledgeFalmer.

Ludema, J., Cooperrider, D. and Barrett, F. (2001) 'Appreciative Inquiry: The Power of the Unconditional Positive Question', in Reason P. and Bradbury, H. (eds) *Handbook of Action Research*. London: Sage Publications, 189–99.

MacIntyre, A. (1981) *After Virtue*, second edition. Notre Dame, IN: University of Notre Dame Press.

Marshall, J. (2001) 'Self Reflective Inquiry Practices', in Reason, P. and Bradbury, H. (eds) *Handbook of Action Research*. London: Sage Publications, 433–99.

Mortiboys, A. (2002) *The Emotionally Intelligent Lecturer*. Birmingham: Staff and Educational Development Association.

Murray, H. G., Gillese, W., Lennon, M., Mercer, P. and Robinson, M. (1996) 'Ethical Principles for College and University Teaching', in Fisch, L. (ed.) *Ethical Dimensions of College and University Teaching: Understanding and Honoring the Special Relationship Between Teachers and Students*. San Francisco, CA: Jossey-Bass.

Palmer, P. (1998) *Courage to Teach*. San Francisco, CA: Jossey-Bass.

Rowland, S. (2000) *The Enquiring University Teacher*. Buckingham: Society for Research into Higher Education/Open University Press.

FURTHER READING

Livsey, R. (1999) *The Courage to Teach: A Guide for Reflection and Renewal*. San Francisco, CA: Jossey-Bass.

MacFarlane, B. (2004) *Teaching with Integrity*. London: RoutledgeFalmer.

Chapter 4

Self-evaluation of your practice

> Evaluation is not primarily about the counting and measuring of things. It entails valuing – and to do this we have to develop as connoisseurs and critics.
>
> (Smith, 2001a)

INTRODUCTION

As children we are taught to learn from others – to observe, imitate and apply. The only time at which we are usually told to learn for ourselves is through our mistakes. This is perhaps why self-evaluation has come to have negative connotations for some of us, or we think that it smacks of navel-gazing or introspection. We fail to associate the term with meaningful learning and development.

Yet, self-evaluation – learning centred on ourselves, our actions and our thoughts – can hold the key to a more authentic and informed development of our practice. The ability to stand back and consider what you do in terms of planning and supporting learning can be immensely valuable to you and your students. Practising without evaluating is a bit like shouting into the darkness: it does not matter how well you shout or how important your message is if you do not know whether anyone is listening. However, there are a number of ways that we can check if anyone is listening – and, more importantly, whether they understand what we are saying.

In this chapter we look at the reasons for evaluating our practice, and the ways in which that process can impact on student learning. This will lead us to consider a number of tools and strategies that allow us to change our understanding of ourselves and our practice, so that we go far beyond mere navel-gazing.

THE WHY, WHAT AND HOW OF EVALUATION

Evaluation is an ongoing process that can help us to identify and illuminate issues within our teaching practice, and alert us to any potential barriers to effective student learning. It allows us to build on the positive aspects of our practice and to address any negative areas. That is the ideal, anyhow; but what about the reality?

The traditional view of evaluation is the standard feedback form, which is circulated to the half-empty final class of the session, where all eyes are fixed firmly on the door and brains are already on vacation. The hastily scribbled-on sheets are collected from seats, desks and floor as the dust settles, an eye is cast over them (perhaps) and they are then filed along with all the other feedback forms. Box ticked, job done. 'Evaluation' comes to be viewed as an event that takes place at the end of something (module, academic year) with a view to satisfying something else (institutional requirement, quality assurance paperwork). Let us think again.

Consider which of the following statements are true, and which are false:

- You can evaluate your practice in a number of different ways.
- Evaluation can happen at any time.
- Evaluation can be quick and easy and still be effective.
- Evaluation can help to develop your teaching.
- Evaluation can be an interesting and enjoyable part of your practice.

You might think that a few of these statements are not generally true: perhaps it is difficult to think of evaluation as enjoyable, or quick and easy; and you might not want evaluation to occur at any point! By adopting a broader and more considered view of evaluation, we aim to demonstrate to you that these statements can all hold. Evaluation can thus break out of the straitjacket and yield genuine benefits, but this will involve moving beyond the 'tick box' approach.

Evaluation can take many forms, sizes and shapes, but this book is concerned with developing *your* teaching. Therefore, our approach to discussing evaluation will be from a personal standpoint that involves you and your practice: self-evaluation. Nonetheless, evaluation does not take place in isolation but is always part of a larger whole. While we may discuss your role as a teacher, for example, this is meaningless without a consideration of student learning. You may teach in the most confident and entertaining of manners, with the potential to speak for hours on end, but if the students are not learning, then something is not quite right. It is no good evaluating one half of the equation, the teaching, without also including the other half, the learning. Although we will refer to *self*-evaluation, it is important to remember that we evaluate ourselves and our teaching within the larger framework of academic practice that includes and involves students, colleagues, our subject area, the institution and so on.

We can focus on many different aspects of our practice. We can consider how well we plan our teaching, put across material to students or design our assessments. There is the nature of our relationships with our students or colleagues at which to look. We can try to make sense of the beliefs and values that underpin our teaching or our emotional state as we teach in a classroom. We can focus on what has gone well, drawing on ideas in the previous chapter from appreciative enquiry, or on what has not worked. We can focus on student feedback or peer review, as discussed in the next chapter; on what is required to demonstrate a case for excellence in teaching, as we will do in Chapter 9; or our ability to introduce an innovation, as we see in Chapter 10. Self-evaluation is typically more effective when we focus on one or more specific elements of our teaching rather than vaguely hope that we will learn something by thinking about ourselves.

Whatever its focus, evaluation involves taking a step back and thinking about the kind of teacher you are currently, the kind of teacher you would like to be and the ways in which you would like your teaching to develop. Evaluating our current practice can tell us about where we are now, but more importantly it can support us in moving towards being the kind of teacher that we would like to be in the future. To achieve this we need to do more than just look at our practice as related to us via a feedback form and then file it for posterity. We need to engage actively in some way with the information. One of the ways you can set about this process is by developing and cultivating a more *reflective* approach to your practice.

ADOPTING A REFLECTIVE APPROACH

Much is written about reflection in higher education today. The terms 'reflective practice' and 'reflective practitioner' are common currency in textbooks on teaching and learning and courses on academic practice;

but to what extent has the discussion penetrated our consciousness and the ways in which we teach and support learning?

Admittedly, the language of reflective practice can be off-putting. Writings on the subject are various, in both length and quality, and it can prove an elusive concept to grasp where words can only too easily serve to obfuscate rather than clarify. Yet, a good deal of potential value lies within the concept if we can cut through the jargon.

Essentially, reflective practice can be seen as a learning conversation; a method of accounting for ourselves; a critical approach; a way of interpreting the interface between practice and theory; and a post-modernist way of knowing and learning (adapted from Ghaye and Ghaye, 1998). As outlined in Figure 4.1, we can reflect 'for action' (planning carried out prior to engaging with a given situation); 'in action' (responding to and acting on changes within any given situation or, put most simply, 'thinking on our feet'); and 'on action' (reviewing that situation and planning for what we might do next time in light of what we have learned).

Essentially, these are all aspects of learning within and around any given situation. The following example is from one of the authors' own experiences of using these reflective learning positions.

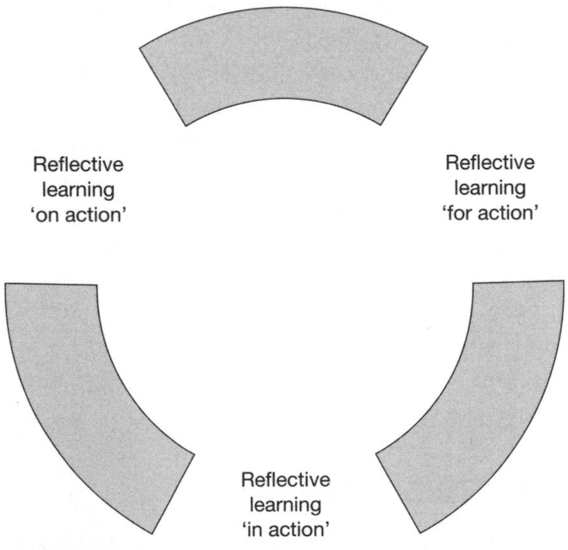

FIGURE 4.1 Aspects of reflective learning

Source: Based on Schön, 1983.

Box 4.1
HORSESHOE, BOARDROOM AND THEATRE

We had experimented with a variety of seating layouts and by the final workshop I was running out of ideas. I thought about what we had used previously, what had worked well and not so well for this group of diverse learners in a class whose size fluctuated unpredictably from week to week. There had been a request from a student to try out a circle shape and I thought about how we would manage this while accommodating the facilitators, overhead projector (OHP) and guest speaker.

The day of the workshop arrived. My original idea of having the facilitators move between the OHP and the middle of the group during the session had to be abandoned, however, as I was unable to join the class at the beginning of the session to set this up. By the time I did arrive the other facilitator had already set up a closed circle, including chairs for both of us. I decided to see how we would manage without using the OHP (now sitting in splendid isolation outside the circle) and to focus our attention on our discussion rather than the screen.

It was the first time I had ever facilitated a session within a closed circle rather than an open horseshoe. How could such a small change make such a difference?! The intensity and richness of the discussion flowed back and forth across the points of the circle, within which the energy seemed almost tangible. Props such as the OHP had been made redundant in the powerful discussion space that had been created. It was a magical teaching moment for me and a key learning experience.

There are a number of frameworks that can help us to appreciate the practical value of this reflective approach when applied to evaluation. One of the most popular is Kolb's model, based on Lewin's four-stage cycle of adult learning, which recognises that development and change is a non-linear, cyclical process dependent on both our ability to learn effectively and our willingness to implement that change. A variant of this model is outlined in Figure 4.2.

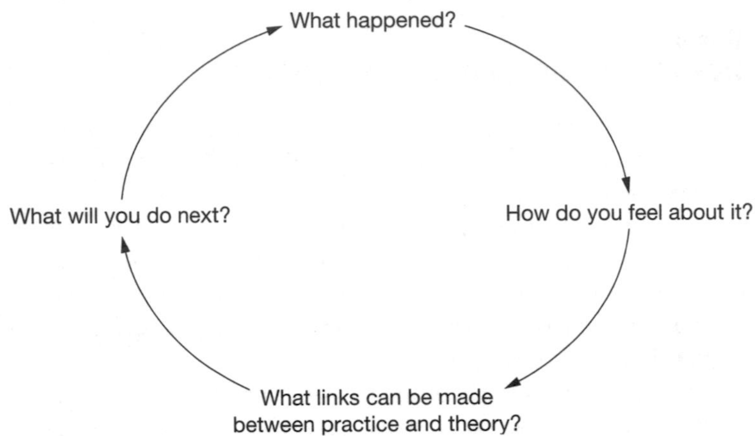

FIGURE 4.2 A cyclical view of learning from experience

Source: Adapted from Kolb, 1984.

Each stage of the cycle is important, influencing the degree of criticality that we are able to bring to bear on our teaching:

- *What happened?* Learning is unlikely to result from a cursory glance at some aspect of your teaching, whether it is represented to you on a student feedback form or through your own memory. We need to embody the experience in a genuinely rich fashion, perhaps in a detailed written description or commentary to a colleague.
- *How do you feel about it?* The concrete expression of the experience provides a genuine basis to observe what occurred, enabling us to look at the experience from a variety of different angles or viewpoints, perhaps in light of a specific methodology.
- *What links can be made between practice and theory?* We may then perceive patterns and meaning within the experience, enabling us to connect the experience to concepts and theories. This richness of understanding helps us to appreciate the need for change and suggests ways forward.
- *What will you do next?* We can then employ this understanding to guide us in making changes in our practice, experimenting with new possibilities; enabling us to engage in further experiences.

Case study 4.1, from Melissa Highton, demonstrates how we can use Kolb's model as a structured framework to help us learn from our experiences. Also note how Melissa is actually working here with 'double loop' learning (Argyris and Schön, 1974), as she has gone through one iteration of the learning cycle already (see her comments within the context-setting section), which she then follows with this cycle in order to deepen and enrich her learning – and to develop her teaching.

Case study 4.1
THE LEARNING CYCLE

Context

I teach on a postgraduate module that looks at using technology in teaching. While feedback on the module in previous years has been good, comments are often characterised by conflicting views on the value of changing teaching to include new e-learning technologies. It was this feedback, and thinking about how I might respond to it, that made me rethink and plan a new approach to designing an online task for the group. The task was designed specifically to acknowledge polarisation of views and challenge participants to back up their opinions with more than anecdotal evidence.

What did you do?

I designed an online task in the shape of a formal debate on a given motion 'This house believes . . .'. In this case the motion concerned the amount of time required by staff to implement technology in teaching, an issue that is of real concern to module participants. The debate lasted six weeks. The asynchronous nature of the debate online ensured that time was given to participants to prepare and reflect on postings and to gather evidence from materials covered as the module progressed. Participants were given specific roles and responsibilities, and everyone in the group submitted evidence to the debate.

How did you feel about it?

In reflecting on this experience I can identify the value of the experiment on several levels. Not only was I able to respond to feedback regarding the need to recognise a range of views among the participants but I could also ensure that those views were expressed and challenged within the group with everyone having an equal voice. An unexpected outcome was that it was also a good classroom management tool as I was able to give specific roles to dominant characters in the group and create a place (the online debate chamber) where views could be 'heard' and recorded.

What links can be made between practice and theory?

I recognise the importance of demonstrating how examples of technology can be used in teaching and learning. In this task I was able to demonstrate how asynchronous discussion rooms can be integrated within a face-to-face module as part of a blended learning approach. Moreover, when the class were discussing the theory of designing and assessing online discussions and use of the institutional virtual learning environment, we were able to refer to what had been happening in the debate in previous weeks.

What will you do next?

The outcome has been to create a lasting resource of links and material to which participants can refer in preparing their assignments and to which I can refer in designing the module for the following year. I plan to facilitate a similar debate – with a different motion – again this year.

Melissa Highton, Staff and Departmental Development Unit, University of Leeds

In order to learn effectively from our self-evaluation we need to begin to adopt a more critically evaluative stance in order to move us past the stage of tending to experience what we believe we will experience in any given learning situation (Cell, 1984, cited in Moon, 2004: 117). Developing a more reflective approach to our practice can help us achieve this, as can working with others. You may have received the impression so far that self-evaluation is a solitary business, during which you sit down in a room on your own and try to recall and make sense of something. It can indeed be like this, but self-evaluation can still involve others, and some of the richness that is required for reflective learning may result from interactions with colleagues or students. Indeed, feedback plays a very important role in supporting us in taking effective learning from self-evaluation.

In Case study 4.1 we can see how the student feedback prompted Melissa to review and develop her teaching in a particular direction in order to better support student learning. Without the benefit of that feedback, Melissa may have refocused her teaching in a way that failed to connect with the students' learning. The use of feedback as a learning tool will be considered in greater detail in the next chapter, but at this point it is worth considering the ways in which other people can prompt you to consider issues that you only too easily can overlook, including providing you with an audience to whom you can suggest possible courses of action.

The challenge remains, however, actually to apply our understanding of the theoretical knowledge to our own practice. Perhaps your own discipline has developed ways to focus explicit attention on some aspect of a situation or problem, and you can adapt this method to apply it to your own practice. Alternatively, we can draw on the experience of others who have already begun to do this. In the rest of this chapter, we will look at a number of tools that have already been devised to evaluate our practice.

TOOLS TO SUPPORT SELF-EVALUATION

We consider here a number of tools to support self-evaluation and learning:

- assumption hunting
- action planning
- keeping a learning log or journal
- learning styles questionnaires
- action-oriented tools.

We could consider other tools, but in many ways the important issue is to develop an awareness of which sorts of approach work best for you, and in which contexts. For instance, some of these tools focus more on a rational approach, which carefully analyses practice or plans for subsequent practice, while others allow learning to emerge in a more open fashion. With such a personal understanding, you will then be better placed to determine whether to adopt other tools that you encounter.

Assumption hunting

Assumption hunting (Brookfield, 1995) involves consciously adopting a critically reflective stance towards the underpinnings of your practice. The idea is to hunt down your assumptions or the aspects of your practice that you take for granted, such as presumptions about what constitutes 'good' teaching or strategies that support student learning. Try it for yourself.

Our assumptions can colour our everyday practice even though we advocate different attitudes and approaches. Argyris and Schön (1974) acknowledged this situation by referring to our 'espoused theories' versus our 'theories in use'. Argyris and Schön argued that we all have 'mental maps' that guide us in our actions in any given situation, and that these can be quite different to the theories that we say we follow. For example, we might attempt to rationalise our behaviour by drawing on a theoretical perspective – let us say our use of lecturing as the mainstay of our teaching practice – which, we argue, relates to effective working with large classes. However, our theory in use might

Box 4.2
ASSUMPTIONS

Draw up a list of teaching-related issues about which you think you may already hold assumptions (e.g. it would be impossible to introduce interactive teaching methods into my lecture class of over 100 students):

1 Consider your list. Now look beyond these immediate responses – what do you find underneath? (e.g. I don't think my students would respond to interactive teaching methods in the lecture setting and I might lose control of the class).

2 Check the validity of your assumptions by discussing them with colleagues (e.g. what experiences your colleagues have had in making their teaching more interactive when working with large groups).

3 Check the validity of your assumptions again by observing your students more closely, talking with them and implementing alternative teaching and learning strategies (e.g. try introducing some pair work or small-group problem solving within some of your lectures. What worked well and what could have been improved? Ask your students!).

P.S. Continue to check your assumptions on a regular basis!

Adapted from Zachary, 2000.

be quite different, in that we use lecturing as our only teaching methodology because we are too busy and stressed to think about what else we might do with a large group of students.

Smith (2001b) argues that reflection has a key role to play here in revealing the theory in use and in exploring the way in which it relates to our espoused theory. The gap in itself does not pose a problem – unless it grows too large – but a connection between the two 'creates a dynamic for reflection and for dialogue'. Such 'double-loop' learning arises from developing an in-depth awareness and knowledge about what we think and how we act. Consequently, assumption hunting has a key role to play in our practice when we encounter any new teaching and learning situation. It can also be an enlightening exercise to carry out *with* your students.

Action planning

Action planning provides you with the opportunity to evaluate your current position and to use that information to plan for your future development. It is based around a structured framework of questions that guides you through the process of self-evaluation, reflection and planning. The structured nature of the questions supports you in addressing all aspects of the planning, as the sequence of questions follows on logically one from the other, without allowing you to avoid any potentially difficult or challenging aspects! Table 4.1 is an example of what that framework might look like.

Planning a clear strategy and approach towards developing your teaching links directly to your ability to support student learning. For example, there is little immediate use in attending events or undertaking training courses with a focus on distance learning if all of your scheduled teaching for the next year is centred around lectures and lab work. However, you might want to include developing your skills in teaching at a distance as a longer-term goal if that is the direction in which you would like to move. Your immediate goals, however, would need to focus on developing your lecturing and facilitation skills. Putting your short-term and long-term goals down on paper in a structured way, whether it is in table form, a diagram or a drawing, can help you to make links and to see opportunities. For example, undertaking a staff development course on planning teaching sessions will support you in developing your lectures now, but can also be used to stimulate your thinking about how you might deliver that same session at a distance.

TABLE 4.1 Action planning framework

What kind of teacher am I now?	
What are my roles and responsibilities?	
What does my personal philosophy of teaching look like?	
What kind of teacher do I want to be?	
Who are my role models?	
What are my aspirations?	
Where do I see myself in five years' time? What will I be doing?	
How will I get there?	
What are my short-term goals? And long-term?	
What resources are available to support me in achieving my goals? How can I access them?	
What might inhibit me from realising my goals?	

Keeping a learning log or journal

Keeping a learning log or journal can help you to carry out a self-evaluation of your practice over a longer period of time. Recording your thoughts in this way provides a 'vehicle for reflection' (Moon, 1999: 4) that can facilitate ongoing review and opportunities for development of your practice. In order to maintain the momentum, keep the entries concise. Use drawings, diagrams or bullet point lists – anything that makes the exercise maintainable and meaningful for you. In order to get started you might think about working around a structure such as:

- What happened?
- What did I learn from that incident?
- How have I been able to apply that learning to my practice?

A log or journal can support you in reviewing where you were in relation to your practice at a particular time, how far you have developed, and what strategies or approaches supported that development. You can also reflect on why your practice has developed in a particular way or style, or why it has not developed as much as you had planned, or differently from what you had anticipated. On beginning a course on teaching and learning, you might find it useful to keep such a log, which will then allow you to review your progress over the course of your studies. In your first year of teaching, you might consider keeping a log that could include details of your teaching sessions, your thoughts on how the sessions went and what you might do the next time that you have to give that particular lecture, encounter that same group of students or have to think about delivering that complex topic in a stimulating and interesting way. Regardless of how experienced we become as teachers, there is always value in maintaining some form of log, perhaps to capture a special moment or to record your response to a challenging situation. We think that we will remember these important events, but it is all too easy for them to slip away unnoticed amidst our hectic lives.

Learning styles questionnaires

Learning styles questionnaires can provide you with an insight into your preferred style of learning. Developing an awareness of how we learn, and the ways in which that process informs and relates to how we teach, can support us in understanding and developing our practice. There are a number of different styles of questionnaire that you can complete, and your choice of questionnaire might provide the first clue to your personal learning style!

Perhaps the most well known is the Honey and Mumford (1992) questionnaire, which identifies four learning styles: activist (those who prefer to learn by doing); reflector (those who prefer to think and observe before taking action); pragmatist (those who want to put their learning into practice in the 'real world'); and theorist (those who like to understand the theoretical perspectives behind their actions). A different range of categories is presented by the VARK questionnaire (www.vark-learn.com/english/index.asp), which is based on the following range of sensory modalities: visual, aural/auditory, read/write and kinaesthetic. Visual learners are said to respond best to charts, graphs and flow charts, etc.; aural learners prefer spoken information;

a read/write preference means that you will learn best when material is presented in a text-based format; while a kinaesthetic learner relates most to real or simulated practice and experience.

Carrying out a learning styles questionnaire can be a very helpful learning tool for you to use in finding out how you are developing as a teacher, and continuing to develop as a learner. It can also be a very useful exercise to carry out with a new group of students in order to give them insight into their own learning styles and for you to develop an appreciation of the variety of learning styles that you may encounter in your class. In Case study 4.2 Stuart Mackay discusses the impact that carrying out a learning styles questionnaire has had on his practice.

Case study 4.2
IDENTIFYING MYSELF AS A LEARNER

In the spirit of self-development, I tested myself using Honey and Mumford's classic learning styles questionnaire. This identifies the type of 'learning person' you are. They describe four types of learner: theorist, pragmatist, reflector and activist. You may score quite highly in one area and lower in others, identifying strongly with one or more learning styles. However, if you score highly on each of the four styles, it indicates that you have the potential to adapt to different learning situations and to become a more effective learner. The questionnaire can therefore help you to identify your strengths and potential weaknesses as a learner.

The results surprised me as they described me as unassertive, having no 'small talk', being intolerant of anything subjective or intuitive, impatient with waffle and task-oriented rather than people-oriented. This 'other' perspective on my identity was a key learning point as I did not see myself like this! But I came to realise that I was currently spending a lot of my time and energy on tasks – writing reports, replying to emails, reading university policies, marking, etc. If I went to a meeting, I found myself not stopping to chat with colleagues at the end but rushing off in order to return to my tasks. This reflection made me 'see' myself in a different way and I realised what I had become.

I was therefore in a position to change this, and I now spend more time and energy listening and speaking to colleagues and getting to know people at work as individuals. This has helped me in my working relationships with others and has made my work more enjoyable.

Stuart Mackay, Directorate of Radiography, Salford University

Action-oriented tools

Action-oriented tools provide quick and easy ways to get a 'snap-shot' evaluation of both your teaching and, more importantly, the extent of student learning, providing further material on which you can reflect:

Post-it exercise

This method of evaluation provides an instant snapshot of student response to your classes, your teaching and student learning. It can be used with large and small groups.

At the end of a teaching session distribute a number of post-its. Depending on the size of the class, this could be to every student or to a random sample. Ask them to write down something that you would like to know more about, for example: what they have learned from the session; three good things about the class; something that they feel is missing from the class; or their reaction to a new aspect of the class (group work, role play, etc.). Ask the students to stick their anonymous post-its to a designated space (desk, wall or whiteboard) as they leave the room. You can then collect them, stick them in a notebook (including the date, time and nature of the class) and then review them at a convenient time.

So far, so good. But what can you do with your findings? If you discover a number of students returning sketchy, incomplete or blank post-its in response to the question 'What have you learned from today's class?', this will rightly set off a few alarm bells. Initial actions in response to this finding might be: to revisit your learning outcomes and use them more proactively; or to think about the structure of the class and the approaches you might take to support student learning, such as providing a clear overview of the session, making links to previous learning, introducing problem-solving activities and providing 'safe' opportunities for discussion, clarification and questioning; or to make time for a more structured conclusion or summary of the class, perhaps including opportunities for students to contribute to it.

In order to encourage your students to provide a useful response, and in order not to alienate them from this activity, remember to:

- allow time within the allotted class period to complete the activity (five minutes will be sufficient);
- not use this method at the end of every class.

Aeroplanes

This is a fun way to end a session that provides not only you but everyone in the group with an indication of how the class as a whole feels about the session. This method works with any size of group that is able to sit in a closed circle.

Provide everyone with a sheet of paper and ask them to write down a comment in relation to that teaching session. When all the students have done this, ask them to make a paper aeroplane, and send it off into the middle of the circle. Then ask a number of people to select an aeroplane (not their own) and read out the comments.

Follow up the comments with an open question to the group as a whole. Even the most simple of statements can provide a way into deeper discussion and richer feedback. For example, 'I enjoyed the class today' could be followed up with a question such as: 'I'm glad someone has enjoyed the class today. If anyone else feels the same, can they share with us why that is?' This approach can work particularly well with negative comments. For example, 'I hated the role play', could be followed with: 'I'm concerned that someone feels so strongly about the role play in today's class. If anyone else feels the same, can they share with us why that is?'

As with the post-it exercise, the anonymity of this evaluation method provides a 'safe' opportunity for students to express themselves in a genuine way. However, the aeroplane exercise takes us beyond the initial expression of how students feel about something to the reasons why they feel a particular way about an aspect of the class, and this provides us a with a way into how that aspect might be built on, if it is a positive feeling, or altered, if it is negative. Remember to allocate sufficient class time for this exercise in order to gain the maximum benefit from it.

Traffic lights

This evaluation method uses post-its again, but in a way that allows for ongoing discussion and review by both tutor and students. This method works best if it can be continued over the period of a course or a module, with a small to medium-sized group. You will also need to be able to protect some space within the teaching room over the duration of the course, so discuss this with teaching colleagues and/or janitorial staff as appropriate.

Identify your protected space. Ideally this will be a movable whiteboard or flipchart stand that can be put in a corner when others are using the room. Alternatively, it could be a wall, cupboard door, etc. Divide the space into three areas – stop, continue and watch. This translates into red, green and amber in traffic-light parlance! Get hold of several packs of post-its that most closely resemble these colours, and at the end of the first session ask the students to identify by coloured post-it, in the appropriate section, what aspects of the course they would like you to continue, stop or watch (i.e. 'keep an eye on'). Explain to the students that as the course continues they are free to add to, reallocate or remove the post-its. Make clear that you will also remove post-its as issues are addressed. You might also want to consider adding a 'discuss' area into which both you and individual students could move post-it comments that were felt to warrant further discussion before any action is taken.

This method is an excellent way in which to encourage student participation and ownership of their learning. As with all of these evaluation methods, the value lies not only in eliciting immediate reaction from the students but in the potential for immediate response from the tutor. Meaningful and thoughtful comments are more likely to be forthcoming if the response from the tutor has an immediate impact and does not just benefit next year's group.

CONCLUSION

It now remains for you actually to adopt one or more of these tools, or to apply some of the insights from this chapter, in your own practice. If we are to improve our own ability to evaluate our teaching, then we need to see what works for us, and there is no better way to do this than to try things out. You might like to begin by thinking about the approaches to self-evaluation set out in Table 4.2 that can help you to create situations for review and reflection, and how you might act on each of these points in your everyday practice.

TABLE 4.2 Approaches to self-evaluation

Approach to self-evaluation	For example . . .
Question and challenge familiar practice *Our teaching can involve us in repetitive patterns of practice. Don't let that repetition result in a stale and dull approach.*	• How can a tired lecture format be refreshed? • What new ideas can you use to begin your teaching sessions and to capture students' attention?
Problematise teaching and learning *Don't accept your actions and student reactions as inevitable. Put your practice 'under the microscope' and research an aspect of your teaching.*	• Identify an area of your practice that you would like to understand better e.g. why do my students react negatively to carrying out pre-reading for class? • How can I get my students to engage in group discussion?
Adopt a wider perspective *Situate your self-evaluation within a wider context.*	• Evaluate a teaching approach that you use *across* the courses on which you teach. • Discuss the findings from your self-evaluations with colleagues – particularly those from other disciplines with different teaching and learning approaches.

Source: Adapted from Moon, 2004.

REFERENCES

Argyris, C. and Schön, D. (1974) *Theory in Practice: Increasing Professional Effectiveness*. San Francisco, CA: Jossey-Bass.

Brookfield, S. (1995) *Becoming a Critically Reflective Teacher*. San Francisco, CA: Jossey-Bass.

Cell, E. (1984) *Learning to Learn from Experience*. Albany, NY: University of New York Press.

Ghaye, A. and Ghaye, K. (1998) *Teaching and Learning through Critical Reflective Practice*. London: David Fulton.

Honey, P. and Mumford, A. (1992) *The Manual of Learning Styles*. Maidenhead: Peter Honey.

Kolb, D. A. (1984) *Experiential Learning: Experience as the Source of Learning and Development*. Englewood Cliffs, NJ: Prentice-Hall.

Moon, J. (1999) *Learning Journals: A Handbook for Academics, Students and Professional Development*. London: Kogan Page.

Moon, J. (2004) *A Handbook of Reflective and Experiential Learning: Theory and Practice*. London: RoutledgeFalmer.

Schön, D. (1983) *Educating the Reflective Practitioner*. San Francisco, CA: Jossey-Bass.

Smith, M. K. (2001a) 'Evaluation', *The Encyclopaedia of Informal Education*. Online, accessed 24 September 2005, www.infed.org/biblio/b-eval.htm.

Smith, M. K. (2001b) 'Chris Argyris: Theories of Action, Double-loop Learning and Organizational Learning', *The Encyclopedia of Informal Education*. Online, accessed 24 September 2005, www.infed.org/thinkers/argyris.htm.

VARK learning styles questionnaire. Online, accessed 24 September 2005, www.vark-learn.com/english/index.asp.

Zachary, L. (2000) *The Mentor's Guide: Facilitating Effective Learning Relationships*. San Francisco, CA: Jossey-Bass.

FURTHER READING

Angelo, T. A. and Cross, P. (1993) *Classroom Assessment Techniques*. San Francisco, CA: Jossey-Bass.

Day, K., Grant, R. and Hounsell, D. (1998) *Reviewing your Teaching*. Centre for Teaching, Learning and Assessment, The University of Edinburgh in association with the Universities' and Colleges' Staff Development Agency. Online, accessed 24 September 2005, www.tla.ed.ac.uk/resources/ryt/.

George, J. and Cowan, J. (1999) *A Handbook of Techniques for Formative Evaluation*. London: Kogan Page.

Chapter 5

Learning from others

> To be a real teacher . . . requires that you are able to enter the experience of the other. In order to enter the experience of the other, it is critical to be able to enter the experience of oneself (or, more accurately, one's selves). And so, everything comes down to entering one's own experience. But this apparently idiosyncratic and self-centred focus requires the support of colleagues. It is almost impossible by oneself.
>
> (Mason, 1993)

INTRODUCTION

So far, we have looked at a number of strategies and approaches for developing your teaching. In Chapter 2 we focused on selecting appropriate teaching methodologies; then we sought inspiration for our teaching in Chapter 3; and in Chapter 4, we began to think about the process of self-evaluation and review of our practice. Yet, as Mason identifies above, learning from oneself demands the support of others. While this dependence on others in order to learn from oneself may appear to be somewhat incongruous initially, a wider consideration of the situation can help to place it in context. In order to benefit most effectively from our working environments, we need to recognise and value the potential for learning that exists within the resource that is our colleagues and our students.

Kasl *et al.* (1993) identify four development phases of group, or shared, learning, as shown in Table 5.1.

TABLE 5.1 Phases of shared learning

Phase	Stage of learning
Contained learning	Learning is individualised
Collected learning	Learning is shared
Constructed learning	Learning becomes integrated
Continuous learning	Integrated learning becomes a central, in-built part of developing practice

Source: Adapted from Kasl *et al.*, 1993.

This is a concept that can easily be applied to our teaching practice on a number of levels: informal groups of colleagues, teaching teams, department, discipline area, faculty, institution, etc. The potential for movement through these four phases demonstrates a corresponding increase in the effectiveness of shared learning that eventually becomes a habituated aspect of developing our teaching practice. There are a number of ways in which you can realise shared learning through engaging with others, including:

- critical friends
- observation of teaching
- sharing experience through workplace shadowing or secondment
- student feedback
- involvement in committee and validation panel work
- peer learners on a teaching in higher education programme
- mentors and buddy groups
- appraisal or review
- networking with colleagues.

Over the course of this book we will look at several of these suggestions in greater detail: networking in Chapter 6; mentoring in Chapter 7; and both student feedback and observation of teaching in this chapter. Despite a diversity of approach, these methods all have one thing in common: learning from others by using their feedback, perspectives, ideas, comments and reflections to support you in developing your teaching. The construction of this shared learning, a combination of your experiences, others' input, and your reflections, has enormous potential for the effective development of practice. In order to begin to benefit from a shared learning approach, we need to think about ways that we can begin this process. Let us look first of all at learning from, and with, our students.

LEARNING FROM STUDENTS

Student feedback can be gathered in a number of ways, both formal and informal, including face-to-face discussions, online surveys or the more traditional, paper-based feedback questionnaire. Our main focus here will be on the feedback questionnaire, although we will refer to other methods of gathering student feedback later in the chapter.

The implementation of feedback questionnaires is associated with a number of challenges: the process can become routine, trivialised, and the outcomes are often in danger of being ignored, as we touched upon in the previous chapter. Commonly expressed beliefs concerning student feedback include:

- students only tell you what they think you want to hear;
- students only use feedback forms as an opportunity to complain;
- the kinds of students who give fulsome replies are not representative.

And this is probably only scraping the surface of lecturers' complaints and concerns. Yet, before we all begin to nod sagely in agreement, let us look at the situation from the students' perspective for a moment.

Feedback questionnaires often provide students with little incentive to complete them. Questions such as 'Was I an effective teacher?' or 'How well did I structure the classes?' mean little to students who may never take any more of your classes or perhaps never cross your path again. In order to encourage genuine, and useful, responses from our students, we need to focus on their learning, what *they* have gained from the classes, rather than your teaching. Asking students to rate your teaching is actually asking them to carry out a difficult task for which they have little prior experience and often no wider context within which to situate that experience. It is exceedingly difficult for experienced colleagues to decide on what constitutes excellence in teaching, or good practice, let alone students. Let us consider an example of this in action.

Students can often be heard to voice the opinion that they 'learn' best from lectures. Their conception of learning is based on the transfer theory, where information is transferred from lecturer to student by being 'poured' into empty and waiting student heads (Fox, 1983). The reality is, however, that student heads are not only far from being empty, full as they are with their own experiences and previous learning, but they are often not even present at the lecture. Student affection for lectures is most often realised through the collection of a 'good' set of lecture notes, yet there is very little real learning going on at this point. Therefore, if your students rate your lectures highly, ask yourself why that is (or better still ask your students!). Is it because you are an entertaining speaker, you crack jokes or you have cartoons as a regular part of your PowerPoint presentations? Or you provide multiple copies of handouts to students for their absent friends? Or you are tolerant of latecomers, eating in class or high spirits? While there is nothing intrinsically wrong in being or doing any of these things in our lectures, if we feel it is appropriate, we should not be fooled into thinking that this is where learning lies.

We need to ask the questions, then, that can help us to find out more about how well our students are learning as a result of our teaching, not just how entertaining or enjoyable our lectures may be. The skills, attitudes and learning facilitated by many innovative teaching methods, such as peer assessment or role play, may only be acknowledged and appreciated by students some time after the event, and not immediately after it – and yet this is the point at which they are asked to comment on it. Student antagonism towards a particular teaching method can translate into a hostile response on the feedback form, and it is that negativity to the teaching method that will be evaluated, rather than the seeds of learning that may have been planted. So, rather than ask about the teaching per se, ask about the learning. The focus of our two teacher-centred questions above therefore becomes: 'Were you able to learn effectively in this class?' and 'What made that learning possible for you?' These kinds of questions can help to elicit student responses that will be helpful in developing our teaching, the purpose of which, after all, is to support student learning.

Think carefully not only about what you want to ask but how you want to ask it. Pose questions that are concise, clear and to the point; address only one issue in each question in order to avoid confusion and to avoid receiving an answer to only half the question. Ask about what you want to know, but also ensure that it is within your power to make changes in these areas, e.g. do not ask students if they would prefer a larger, brighter, warmer or cooler teaching room if it is not possible to provide one. Try to avoid very general questions such as: 'What were the three best/worst things about this course?', as you are likely to end up with very general responses, something along the lines of 'the lecturer's dress sense, the person sitting next to me and the view out the window' – perhaps in response to both categories.

Good – and by 'good' we mean honest and thoughtful – student feedback has the potential significantly to enrich and improve our practice. In Case study 5.1, Fatosh Gozalpour discusses the insight he gained into student learning from using a feedback questionnaire with a group of international students.

Case study 5.1
ASKING QUESTIONS ABOUT STUDENT LEARNING

Delivering a Master's level engineering course in Qingdao, China, I took the opportunity to implement a questionnaire on approaches to studying. The course was based upon distributed learning, and I was only out in China with the students for one week. Thirteen out of the sixteen students in the group returned their questionnaire, and the majority of those students demonstrated themselves to be surface learners. This situation had been increasingly apparent from the questions posed by the students in lectures, such as: 'What should I memorise?' and the perennial 'Will this be in the exam?' The questionnaire also highlighted the fact that gaining the qualification, rather than engaging with the learning, was the primary motivating factor among the students, largely the result of their studies being funded by their employer. Yet the questionnaires had also revealed the potential for deeper learning among the students, so I challenged myself to think of ways in which I could support such learning, both in the short term with this particular group of students and in the longer term with subsequent cohorts.

Time was the most pressing issue, particularly as the concentrated week's teaching did not allow for much deviation from 'the script' in order to enable the students to begin to explore issues in greater depth. However, I implemented a number of strategies, including making coherent and positive links between different elements of the course and posing problems and questions which were then revisited the following day. The students responded well to this approach, successfully solving the assigned problems and actively engaging in the discussion. Nonetheless, I still have reservations over the students' motivation, which seemed to be largely focused on mastering exam-type questions rather than broadening their thinking in order to support deeper learning. This experience has raised a number of issues for my teaching, however, aside from the anticipated challenges of supporting learning at a distance, including addressing the issue of international students' approaches to learning and the motivation behind their engagement with their studies. These challenges are now as important in informing my teaching practice as subject content and delivery method.

Fatosh Gozalpour, Institute of Petroleum Engineering, Heriot-Watt University

You may find yourself having to use a standard institutional or departmental questionnaire for some of your teaching but do not let this stop you also using your own methods to elicit the feedback that you need to develop your practice – although this does not mean providing every student with two feedback forms! This will result in questionnaire fatigue and correspondingly poor responses. Consider other approaches, such as online surveys, or more personal and interactive formats, such as staff–student committees and focus groups. Body language, vocal tone and facial expressions often speak more loudly than the written word! Face-to-face contact also means, of course, that you can clarify issues and ask students to expand on particular responses, resulting in a much richer, deeper and more valuable form of feedback. In Case study 5.2, Helen Robson demonstrates how she uses a variety of formal and informal methods, including written feedback and observation of student behaviour and reactions, in order to inform the development of her teaching practice. Note also how Helen actively employs the strategies of reflecting 'in' and 'on' practice, as discussed in Chapter 4, in order to inform her teaching.

Case study 5.2
USING STUDENT FEEDBACK TO INFORM FUTURE PRACTICE

Students will not always say what they liked or disliked about a session or course without prompting; sometimes the only way a teacher may know about the effectiveness of his or her teaching is when the students leave the course – i.e. 'vote with their feet'! I find one of the most effective and immediate ways of improving teaching is actively to look for information from students. Even without being proactive in seeking feedback, it is difficult not to be aware of student behaviour in class (for example, looking puzzled or bored, or talking among themselves).

Apart from the formal evaluation procedures required by the university, when I am teaching I look for three main criteria by which to judge my practice: the students' level of interest in the subject; their level of understanding of the subject; and their response to the teaching method. I can gauge their level of interest in the subject by being aware of their body language and by how many and what sort of questions they ask. I can judge the level of understanding of the subject by both the types of questions asked and the answers provided to my questions. Evaluating my choice of teaching method can be done by noting students' willingness to participate and through the outcomes of assessment.

I then use this information to review and reflect on my teaching in two ways. First, I can adjust my lesson plan during a teaching session in an immediate response to student feedback. This method of thinking on my feet, described by Donald Schön as 'reflection-in-action', means that if it is evident that the students have not understood the material I have just delivered, I think about spending more time on the topic, or explaining it in a different way, before moving on. Second, it involves looking back on a session, or carrying out 'reflection-on-action', and in the light of the experience, amending it for next time, or altering the next session. This would happen if, for example, student feedback suggested that there was not enough interaction, or my presentation had been unclear or uninteresting. By regularly reviewing my practice in this way, and using student feedback to inform and support my development, I feel I am continually improving my teaching.

Helen Robson, Institute of Social Work and Applied Social Studies,
University of Staffordshire

Learning from student feedback can help to inform your practice in a number of ways, including: supporting you in developing a better understanding of how students learn; appreciating what works and what does not in terms of your teaching practice; 'road testing' new teaching approaches; responding effectively to student concerns or anxieties; and validating your current approach to practice. In order to ensure that your requests for feedback are treated seriously, and to provide you with useful and genuine feedback, make sure that you also take the evaluation process seriously. Integrate the process of gathering feedback within your teaching; do not just employ it as a bolt-on or after-thought. At the planning stages of a new course or lecture series, think carefully about what kind of feedback mechanisms would be most appropriate and how you will implement it. Always allow adequate class time for students to complete feedback requests to avoid creating resentment and to encourage active participation; and ensure that your responses are timely. Do not wait until the end of the year, when your current students have moved on, before you make changes.

Students can also benefit from the shared learning experience that can be created by effectively designed feedback methods. Val Fisher in Case study 5.3 discusses how feedback from students on her art and design course illuminated the value-added learning that had developed from their studies.

Case study 5.3
ADDING VALUE TO LEARNING THROUGH FEEDBACK

Lecturers are increasingly being faced with a dilemma. Where it was once possible to conduct small-group sessions and create the ideal learning environment, increasing student numbers and larger groups now present challenges to those traditional models. Faced with one such large class, working in a practice-based art and design subject, I aimed to avoid the passive learning that can take place in lectures through the development of a 'show and tell' sketchbook of development work. However, the challenge was in recreating the learning dynamic of small-group teaching, usually facilitated by a 'flick-through' of the sketchbook, in a lecture class of 40 students. I addressed this issue by photographing the pages to illustrate the development process and showed this as a PowerPoint presentation. Prior to this the students undertook a critique of my designs, and then, unaware of the context of my work, presented their analysis to the group. At the appropriate point in the lecture, I talked them through the designs they had previously analysed. They were pleased to discover that their powers of analysis and deduction were astute, and I was pleased that their feedback indicated that my designs were successful. I did take away some ideas for improvements, though.

The written feedback from students at the end of the lecture was very positive but also significant in that it worked on several levels. I was most interested by the comments about the session from the point of view of lesson planning and particularly the student understanding of pedagogy. The comments indicated that the students had evaluated the session not purely as a learning experience for themselves but from a teaching and learning perspective – how to use visual aids, how to structure a two-and-a-half hour session, how to vary the pace through the use of different methods, how to get the group to interact. They then went on to use what they had learned in the peer-assisted learning scheme where third-year students work with first years. It was a 'red letter' day for me, showing how verbal and written feedback were instrumental in informing student learning about their subject, my own learning about my practice as a designer, my practice as a teacher, and student learning about teaching practice!

Val Fisher, The Arts Institute at Bournemouth

Once you have obtained feedback on your teaching, what next? Consider how you will respond to the feedback. What changes might you make in light of the comments? How can you build on the positive areas? How will you communicate those changes to your students? Perhaps the students' response is not quite what you had anticipated. Dealing with criticism can be difficult but always review student feedback objectively and have a colleague help you in order to carry out this process more effectively. In a group of 99 per cent positive feedback, it is that 1 per cent that will niggle away at you. Put it into perspective. Does that student raise a valid issue? Is it a matter that might be of concern to a wider group? Is the student just making 'a point'? Alternatively, you might want to reflect on the 99 per cent. Is such a positive response an accurate reflection of the student-learning experience in your classes? Have you asked the right questions – are they sufficiently probing, clear and targeted in order to help you find out what you want to know? Think about other feedback mechanisms you might use in future.

Soliciting feedback from our students is one way to obtain feedback on our teaching. Our colleagues, however, provide a further source of information and insight into our practice. Feedback from colleagues can add a new perspective to the process of learning from others, as they provide insights and observations from contemporaries who are also involved in the process of developing their teaching.

LEARNING FROM PEER OBSERVATION

Observation of your teaching can be carried out for a number of reasons and by a variety of different colleagues. You may first encounter it as part of a departmental requirement, where the observer may be your head of department or a peer within a buddy group, or as an aspect of the appraisal or review process, with your line manager as the observer. Peer observation often forms an element of teaching in higher education programmes, where both your tutor and peer learners may be involved in the observations, and then as part of ongoing continuing professional development. Observation of teaching practice can and should, therefore, form part of all stages of your academic career. It should be viewed as a positive and regular aspect of your ongoing development rather than as something to be endured or 'got through'. Actively seek it out if it is not forthcoming. In Case study 5.4, Martin Twiste explains the impact that peer observation has had on the development of his teaching practice.

Case study 5.4
A REAL EYE-OPENER

Having acquired my new post as a lecturer, I decided to become further educated myself. I enrolled on a programme that led to a Postgraduate Certificate in Higher Education Practice and Research. This, I thought, would help me in addressing the issues I had with my own teaching, so that I could better support my students in their learning. Part of the programme was based on teaching observations, and I found out that I was required to take part in five of these! For two of the observations, I had to observe both my mentor and a peer on the programme. For the other three, my mentor, a peer and another teacher of my choice had to observe me. The way I felt about my teaching was that I very much enjoyed giving lectures and found it satisfying when at least some students appeared to understand the material I was trying to get across. Unfortunately, this was probably not the case for the majority of students I was supposed to be educating. So I looked forward to seeing what others did in their teaching practice.

What surprised me most was that none of the lecturers I observed used the 'traditional' approach to lecturing of talking continuously for the full lecture period – which was what I had always done, so far. Instead, they used a much more interactive approach, engaging the students from start to finish. This also appeared to support the students in learning far more effectively than they appeared to do in my lectures. Not surprisingly, after the three lecturers observed me, they were under the impression that the students switched off very early on in my lecture and consequently did not learn very much! Having reflected upon the teaching observations, I decided to implement a much more interactive teaching style within my own practice. This was an astonishing experience, as I soon noticed how much more interested the students were in what I was saying, and how much better they retained the information I presented. This approach to teaching was a real eye-opener for me, and a reflection of the value of having taken part in the teaching observations.

Martin Twiste, Directorate of Prosthetics and Orthotics, University of Salford

While having your teaching observed has a developmental focus, it is also a means of assessing your capability as a teacher, and naturally you will want to be able to demonstrate your skills in the classroom to the best of your abilities. So, what steps can you take to do well in your teaching observation? Think about what you want to achieve. Observation of teaching is a developmental process, so rather than just aiming for a 'pass' and nothing more, you should focus on how you can build on the good aspects of your practice and consider the ways in which you can develop the weaker areas.

Find out what your observer is looking for. As with any assessment, the criteria should be transparent and available to you. It is not 'cheating' to see the criteria against which you will be assessed before the observation is carried out. What it does do is to enable you to reflect on specific aspects of your teaching – for example, your use of body language or voice projection or eye contact with students – and to consider these criteria in relation to your current practice. Some of these aspects may not have occurred to you before, and you may want to flag up to the observer that you are unsure of the extent of your ability in these areas, and that you would particularly appreciate feedback on them. This is not a sign of incompetence but rather a clear signal to your observer that you are aware of both your stronger and weaker areas and that you see the observation as a good opportunity to develop your teaching.

Provide the observer with a lesson plan and background information on the class – level, experience, any students with special needs, etc.

Be clear about what your aims and objectives are for the class and share these with the observer – and the students! Explain whether there will be group-work activities or whether you or the students will be moving around the room. This will influence where the observer will choose to sit. Ask how long the observer intends to stay. A traditional lecture period of 50 minutes should present no problems, but a longer workshop of several hours or perhaps a day's duration will require some negotiation. The observer may choose to stay until a convenient break or activity is introduced into the session.

Do not be tempted to pick your 'best' class for the observation. The aim is not to achieve the ideal teaching session but rather to demonstrate your ability to react to and work with the class, regardless of their level of ability. Much better to be able to demonstrate your strategies for motivating disinterested individuals or supporting students with a wide range of abilities than having the 'perfect' class. Having said that, however, it would be prudent not to choose a class where only one or two students ever turn up or one that centres around a presentation from a student with a notoriously poor attendance rate. Those are issues that can be dealt with at another time! Similarly, avoid flashy presentations with many PowerPoint graphics or numerous links to the web unless you are very confident of your skills in this area (and more importantly your strategies for coping with the situation if the system crashes). Once you have reassured your students that the observer is not there to assess their performance but yours, they do tend to react very positively and supportively. Nonetheless, having another person in your class, particularly in a non-participatory observer's role, will change the dynamic, so be prepared for perhaps less banter or light-hearted exchanges from the students but potentially more effort!

Remember that the observer is exactly that – an observer. Do not ask them to participate in the class or ask them questions. It is good practice, however, to introduce them to the students at the beginning of the class and to remind students as to why the observer is present. Think about where you would like the observer to sit and suggest this to them but also be prepared for the observer choosing a different area of the room. Do not be intimidated by this! It is simply that as a new person to the class, their perspective will be different from yours.

Check out the teaching room in advance of your session (always good practice) to ensure that necessary equipment is both present and functioning. Take some time to consider what you will do if there are technical difficulties during the class or fewer than the expected number of students turn up. Do not fixate on this as a list of potential disasters; developing the habit of reflecting on these kinds of issues is good practice.

Timely feedback is always the most useful. Make sure that you have an opportunity to discuss the session with your observer immediately afterwards or at least the same day. The written feedback can follow later, and a short gap between the session and receiving the write-up can provide time and space for reflection.

You might also like to consider making a video recording of your teaching session. Video recordings of your teaching are particularly useful in that they constitute a permanent record of practice that can be revisited and reviewed, not only by you but also in conjunction with a mentor, buddy or close colleague. Gaining this kind of multiple perspective on your practice provides excellent triangulation. You will have your initial thoughts on your teaching from having experienced it directly. You will then gain a different perspective on your practice by viewing it from the 'students' eye' view via the video. A third perspective will be supplied by your colleague. The cognitive dissonance provided by these multiple perspectives creates a space in which learning and development can occur. For example, you may have felt while delivering your lecture that the structure was clear and comprehensible. On watching the video you may still feel that this is the case but that your distracting hand movements or pocket-change jingling diverts your attention from the lecture altogether. A colleague's comments may reveal other aspects of your practice, both positive and negative, of which you may not have been aware. Discussion can allow you to explore the issues in a range of ways, including identifying patterns of behaviour, exploring alternative actions, and investigating possible underlying reasons behind more challenging aspects of your practice.

In addition to being observed, actively seek out opportunities to observe your colleagues. This could be a mentor, peers on a teaching in higher education programme or perhaps a 'buddy' group or learning set that encourages a number of colleagues to observe each others' teaching. This process could be a formalised part of the development of good practice within a department or teaching team, or it could be a more informal set-up within a group of colleagues. If you do not already have such an opportunity to observe your colleagues' teaching, make a point of actively seeking it out. Begin by asking a close colleague. Try to observe colleagues with differing levels of experience, and also from different discipline backgrounds. Do bear in mind, however, that teaching has traditionally been a largely private activity between teacher and students and that some colleagues may be reluctant to have someone else sit in on their teaching. Raising and discussing the idea of peer observation with your head of department or at a staff meeting, or discussing the literature on the subject, are all ways in which the practice can be introduced.

The feedback that you receive from your teaching observation will – hopefully – be constructive and supportive. However, we should not forget that providing good feedback, centred around constructive criticism, is a skill in itself. Be discriminating. Feedback on your teaching can be very valuable, but you are also dealing here with the values and attitudes of others. They might 'see' things within your teaching that perhaps resonate with potential development areas within their practice, meaning that they unconsciously project those feelings onto you. Always take time to review and discuss feedback – do not react spontaneously without giving it due consideration, perhaps asking for a second opinion from another colleague, or situating your practice within an understanding of the relevant theory. Most importantly, create an action plan. It is important to do this as soon as possible after reviewing the feedback, particularly if you will not be teaching that class, module or course for another year. Do not lose the learning.

CONCLUSION

Learning from others should become an integral part of your practice in order to support the development of your teaching. As teachers, we never stop learning. Indeed, the truth behind the often quoted maxim that you do not really begin to understand something fully until you teach it to others is borne out in lecture theatres, seminar rooms and labs in our institutions on a daily basis. We can learn from students, academic colleagues, support staff and alumni at different times, and in different ways. It is important to be open and receptive to possible learning opportunities from wherever they might come. This may sound like a somewhat passive activity, sitting in wait for a learning opportunity to present itself, but this should not be the case. In addition to developing effective feedback mechanisms and planning to have your teaching observed, and to observe others' teaching, you should also begin to think about other ways in which you can actively seek out opportunities to learn from others. You are probably doing a surprising

Box 5.1
OPPORTUNITIES TO LEARN FROM OTHERS

Engage with the literature on teaching and learning:

- Read the *Times Higher Educational Supplement* (*THES*) every week.
- Sign up for the *Scholarly Articles Research Alerting* (*SARA*) www.tandf.co.uk/sara service, so that you always know when the latest editions of journals are published.
- Check out your library for books on learning, teaching and assessing (also your staff development library if you have one).
- Share and discuss interesting articles with colleagues – provoke debate and discussion.
- Find out whether your institution has an in-house or online journal where staff can contribute – submit an article.

Become involved with a network for teaching and learning:

- Find out whether your institution supports such a network – if not, consider starting one yourself.
- Consider joining a professional association allied to teaching and learning, such as the Higher Education Academy www.heacademy.ac.uk.
- Join an email discussion group appropriate to your teaching and learning interests through JISC mail, www.jisc.ac.uk (see FAQs, which include information on jiscmail).

Attend development events on teaching and learning:

- Participate actively in your institution's staff development programme.
- Look out for relevant conferences and events on teaching and learning – and consider submitting a paper/ workshop/ poster presentation.

amount of this already, but by developing a greater awareness of how you might be doing so, you can build and capitalise on that learning. You can begin this process by reviewing a number of aspects of your academic practice, and the ways in which you can begin to engage with these aspects of practice as outlined below, which all involve learning from others in one way or another. What do you do already? How can you generate more learning from these activities? How can you engage with the other activities?

REFERENCES

Fox, D. (1983) 'Personal Theories of Teaching'. *Studies in Higher Education*, 8, 2, 151–63.

Kasl, E., Dechant, K. and Marsick, V. (1993) 'Internalizing Our Model of Group Learning', in Boud, D., Cohen, R. and Walker, D. (eds) *Using Experience for Learning*. Buckingham: Society for Research into Higher Education/Open University Press.

Mason, J. (1993) 'Learning from Experience in Mathematics', in Boud, D., Cohen, R. and Walker, D. (eds) *Using Experience for Learning*. Buckingham: Society for Research into Higher Education/Open University Press.

FURTHER READING

Schön, D. (1987) *Educating the Reflective Practitioner*. San Francisco, CA: Jossey-Bass.

Webb, G. (1994) *Making the Most of Appraisal: Career and Professional Development Planning for Lecturers*. London: Kogan Page.

Chapter 6

Working with others

> I walked along the corridor towards the lecture theatre. It was my first time. The dull roar of voices, laughter, and banging of seats got louder and louder and more and more terrifying. I opened the door and was greeted by row upon row of faces; inquisitive, bored, sniggering, staring, like something out of a street scene by Hogarth. Years of solitary confinement as a researcher hadn't prepared me for this.

INTRODUCTION

Despite being surrounded by hundreds of students, often all at the one time, teaching can be a very isolated experience. Traditionally, academics were appointed as researchers who would also do a little teaching on the side in their own specialism, and would have prepared and delivered their lectures with little thought of discussion with other colleagues. That situation has long gone. Working with others has become a cornerstone of academic life and colleagues, peers and students have become increasingly important to our teaching practice in terms of collaborative work, evaluation, feedback and development. We now work in a teaching and learning environment that is increasingly focused on team effort, interdisciplinary working, subject-related networks and sharing of practice. Some of these groupings appear to come 'ready-made' while others have to be created and supported through networking and the development of peer groups and contacts. All of them have to be nurtured and maintained.

This chapter looks at a number of ways in which you can develop collaborative approaches to developing your teaching. The first of these is networking. We consider the many benefits of becoming a proactive and effective networker and the ways in which this can be achieved. Then we look at communities of practice, going behind the jargon to establish what is meant by the term and how you can become involved in these communities. Finally, we discuss working in a team, and the ways in which this kind of collaborative practice can support the development of your teaching.

NETWORKING

Hectic teaching schedules, endless meetings, marking, deadlines and piles of paperwork. These are only some of the reasons that can prevent you from interacting and networking with your colleagues. Yet, networking is a key aspect of an academic's working life, which can often result in support, advice or direct help that can impact on how we deal with the more demanding and challenging aspects of our practice. Networking is important to everyone's career development, but it can be particularly important if, for example, you are on a part-time or fixed-term contract, your office is not centrally located on campus or you spend a lot of time working independently, when it can be all too easy to be missed out of the information loop. Begin to think about the role that networking plays in your working life by considering these review questions:

- Consider the people you have contact with in your professional life. Which would you regard as your immediate circle and what function do these individuals play in your working life?
- What about the next circle? And the next?
- How many circles are there?
- Are you aware of whether the circles overlap – and is this important to you?
- Do you actively seek out new networks and acquaintances?
- How can you do this better?

A network, or networks, of colleagues can open a number of routes to more effective working. Here are some suggestions for how that can work in practice:

- learning from others' successes and failures in teaching;
- raising your visibility and your profile as a teacher;

- getting a feel for the 'politics' of a situation;
- broadening your knowledge of teaching and learning;
- getting your name known in your institution;
- receiving invitations to give guest lectures/act as an external examiner/sit on a validation panel;
- developing your national and international reputation/profile in your discipline area;
- keeping abreast, or ahead, of developments and trends in teaching and learning – or beginning to set them yourself;
- finding out about and understanding how university systems work;
- finding out what others think about teaching and learning issues – peers, senior colleagues, the sector, different disciplines;
- developing and disseminating good practice;
- problem solving;
- sharing and validating learning;
- getting to know who is who.

Many of these activities will make your work more interesting and enjoyable, but they can also support the development of your teaching through sharing of practice, ideas and information. They can also potentially lead to promotion and advancement through opportunities to develop and enhance your expertise and academic reputation.

When people start to discuss networking, they often think automatically of conferences, writing papers and related costs in both time and money, and they feel overwhelmed. Conferences can be great for networking if you make best use of the opportunities – more on this later – but before you reach this point there are any number of smaller things that you can do to get started. There are many ways of beginning to network effectively, from your very first days in post in a new job, including attending organised events such as induction for new staff, joining a reading group, the sports centre or musical society, or perhaps creating your own personal web page and linking to colleagues' sites. All of these approaches will involve you in four key aspects of good networking practice:

- being proactive
- getting involved

- letting people know who you are
- making connections.

Here are some further suggestions to help you network:

- join, and contribute to, email discussion lists;
- collect colleagues' business cards;
- have your own business cards printed – and distribute them;
- identify common interests with colleagues;
- visit other institutions;
- invite colleagues from other institutions to visit you;
- find a mentor;
- set up a buddy group;
- join an action learning set.

As you can see, there are a number of different levels at which you can begin to network. Consider the following review points and make a commitment to do at least one thing this week from both the departmental and institutional levels lists. Also, think about how you might begin to network proactively at a national or international level.

Review point 6.1
DEPARTMENTAL NETWORKING

1 Get out and about around the corridors meeting people.

2 Smile and say hello as you pass colleagues in the corridor – make an impact.

3 Go to the coffee room, lunch canteen or common room and do not sit on your own – introduce yourself and ask if you can join colleagues already seated.

4 Make sure that your name is on your door – if you have to wait for an official nameplate, make a temporary one for yourself.

5 Invite colleagues to coffee or lunch – find out about their subject areas and interests.

Review point 6.2
INSTITUTIONAL NETWORKING

1 Think vertically as well as horizontally.

2 Join committees relevant to your field of study and interests – find out how your institution 'works'.

3 Explore opportunities for secondment to other areas of the university, such as learning support or disability centres, which could enhance your skills development.

4 Participate in, or consider running, staff development sessions – a great way to meet new colleagues in addition to developing your skills.

5 Investigate the possibility of shadowing senior colleagues.

6 Attend institutional events, introduce yourself and speak with colleagues.

7 Attend conferences at national and international levels, which provide excellent networking opportunities.

Aim to build up a variety of networks. You will find that some of these will be focused on a particular group of people such as colleagues in your discipline area, while others will have a more diverse composition, and might include colleagues working in a variety of areas, such as: using information technology to support student learning; employing different approaches to teaching such as problem-based learning or Objective Structured Clinical Examinations (OSCEs); or an interdisciplinary group looking at ways to develop inter-professional learning. You might also find yourself becoming involved in networking groups that have a more specific agenda that may lean more towards lobbying or political activism, or a group that adopts a particular standpoint, such as supporting women or ethnic minorities in academia.

Is it a good idea to become involved in these activist groups? They can be highly supportive and they provide a 'safe' forum for discussion, but they can also arouse hostility or suspicion from others excluded from that group, particularly if you are successful in achieving your aims. It would be inadvisable to restrict yourself to one kind of group, and working on developing a broad range of contacts and networks will avoid this. As you develop more extensive networks of peers, colleagues and contacts, you will find yourself gravitating naturally towards those with which you identify most closely. This development will lead on to involvement in communities of practice.

Review point 6.3
(INTER) NATIONAL NETWORKING

1 Always aim to present rather than just attend – it is often cheaper to participate as a presenter and you will have better opportunities to network with the conference organisers.

2 Start by offering poster presentations – this provides the opportunity to meet and chat with potentially all of the participants rather than the self-selected few who may choose to listen to a paper.

3 Check the delegate list at an early stage – aim to speak with a wide variety of participants.

4 Do not feel that you have to attend all the sessions – your time may be spent more profitably in chatting informally with other participants.

5 Exchange business cards/email addresses/contact details with a range of colleagues.

6 After the conference, send a brief email to everyone who you would like to keep in contact with.

COMMUNITIES OF PRACTICE

The movement from personal networking to involvement in communities of practice can be seen as part of a continuum that also embraces the concept of critical collaboration and critical communities – see Figure 6.1.

In order for collaborative working to have an effective and insightful impact on our teaching, we need to adopt a critical stance and to approach it in a way that is objective and analytical. Working with others provides a range of opportunities for critique, analysis and evaluation of our practice that should not be shunned in favour of a 'cosy'

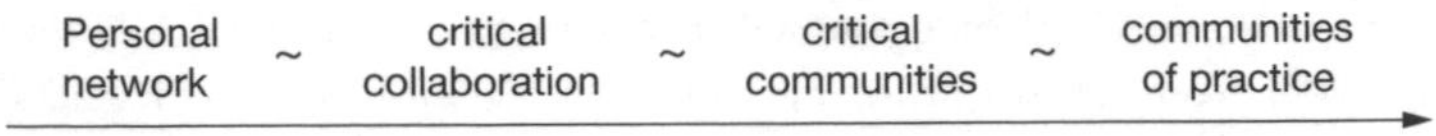

Personal network ~ critical collaboration ~ critical communities ~ communities of practice →

FIGURE 6.1 Continuum of practice from personal networking to communities of practice

relationship that results in little being explored or examined and nothing moving forward. Such collaboration can be created and fostered within a range of critical communities.

Critical communities can take a number of forms and can involve many different individuals, depending on the purpose of the group. The critical community moves the centre of attention from the individual experience to that of the group, forming a focus for debate, examination of practice and learning (Campbell *et al.*, 2004). Such groups tend to join together for time-limited periods in order to focus on a particular topic. Examples of critical communities include research groups, working groups and peer groups within organised programmes of study. The strength of these critical communities lies in the range of knowledge, interest and desire to further understanding and share learning, as a result of critical engagement and discussion through collaborative working, of the group's participants. Critical communities can also be created on a more personal level by individuals seeking to engage with

TABLE 6.1 Suggestions for critical communities

For teaching	For research into teaching	For continuing professional development
• Mentor • Peer • Senior colleague • Teaching Fellow • Email discussion group • Students	• Fellow teacher researcher • Link with Higher Education Academy subject centre in your discipline area • Research mentor • Students	• Staff development officer • Mentor • Colleagues working in the areas in which you would like to develop • PG teaching in higher education programme

Source: Adapted from Campbell *et al.*, 2004.

critical debate in order to examine a particular idea, issue or concern within their practice. The success of this kind of critical community depends heavily on personal networks. A variation on this model of working together is the action learning set, although the focus here is more on group mentoring than on critique. Table 6.1 demonstrates the range of colleagues that might be involved, and the links that can be made, to create a variety of critical communities to support the development of your practice.

The benefits of working together in this way include:

- triangulation;
- multiple views from a variety of perspectives;
- interdisciplinary working.

In Case study 6.1, David Potter explains how his engagement with a 'critical community' provided by his participation in a Postgraduate Certificate in Academic Practice programme supported him in engaging with a new technology in order to make a significant impact on his practice.

Case study 6.1
SUPPORTING LEARNING THROUGH ENGAGING WITH A CRITICAL COMMUNITY

My initial encouragement to develop online material came as a result of working with a group of international distance learning students. I had delivered a one-week intensive course to the students and now needed to provide them with relevant assignment tasks that would help them focus on the course material in the intervening months until they sat the exam. I was motivated to do this partly through learning about virtual learning environments (VLEs) as part of my studies on a Postgraduate Certificate in Academic Practice (PGCAP) programme.

One of the five modules comprising the PGCAP was devoted to e-learning and hands-on experience of using our institution's choice of VLE, WebCT. It soon became apparent that there were a number of advantages in using a VLE to complement my traditional face-to-face teaching methods. For me, the main advantage of the VLE was that I could post large files, such as detailed plots of data, that were difficult either to send to the students via email or to give them in hard-copy format. It also meant that each student could work with extended log intervals in full colour rather than printed black and white copies of selected sections (the latter being necessary in the traditional approach with a large class of students). Other features, such as the use of animations to explain the workings of some of the tools, were added advantages.

The VLE provided a practical solution for me to post relevant tasks, for the students to post their answers and for me to deliver feedback. My learning on the PGCAP programme also helped me in the design of the tutorials, and in the assessment and feedback on the assignments. It later turned out that the students who completed the online tutorials in general performed significantly better in the exams than those who did not undertake the tutorials. This has now prompted me to make similar supplementary material available for all my students, allowing me to manage more effectively my traditional teaching time and material, and to enhance the learning experience for my students.

David Potter, Institute of Petroleum Engineering, Heriot-Watt University

We all belong to a range of different academic communities – our department, faculty, institution, etc. – and you may associate this with, or describe it as, your 'community of practice'. The nature of these units, in terms of membership, aims and identity, can be quite different, however, from the groupings identified within the literature as communities of practice, as is demonstrated in Table 6.2.

We can see from Table 6.2 that the two most similar professional groupings are personal networks and communities of practice. The other groups have much more defined and inflexible structures, membership and purpose. Some of them even have conflicting and potentially confusing and challenging features, for example, departments, which are both hierarchical and collegiate, and competitive as well as developmental. Networks and communities of practice, on the other hand, are much more fluid, developmental and supportive.

So, can communities of practice be seen as an extension of personal networks? In many ways, they can. 'Communities of practice', like personal networks, develop around areas in common – knowledge, expertise and specialisms. Such groupings develop, share and implement development both within discrete areas of practice and across institutional and international boundaries. Involvement in them, and identification with them, becomes a logical extension of personal networks. Personal networking centres around you, the individual, whereas a community of practice centres around a group identity.

TABLE 6.2 Academic professional groupings

Professional grouping	Group membership	Group purpose	Group boundaries	Group features
Personal networks	Self-selected	Develops and supports elements of practice	Fluid	Non-hierarchical, supportive, sharing, focused on learning and development
Departments	Appointed	Delivery and furtherance of departmental aims and objectives	Defined	Hierarchical, collegiate, competitive, developmental
Faculties	Appointed	Delivery and furtherance of faculty aims and objectives	Defined	Hierarchical and collegiate
Institutions	Appointed	Delivery and furtherance of institutional aims and objectives	Defined	Hierarchical or collegiate
Communities of practice	Self-selected	Develops and supports elements of practice	Centred around a negotiated identity	Non-hierarchical, collaborative culture

Source: Adapted from Wenger *et al.*, 2002 and Trowler and Knight, 2000.

Now that we know more about what constitutes a 'community of practice', what benefits can we gain from engaging with them? Working within a community of practice can:

- facilitate integration into an academic community;
- reduce isolation and the feeling that you are the only person experiencing particular challenges;
- provide a legitimate voice for an issue or concern;
- enable access to 'embedded' or tacit knowledge systems;
- send messages and achieve goals;
- provide a forum in which to act 'politically';
- construct and reconstruct personal and professional identity;
- send messages about you through your activity and involvement.

Examples of a formal community of practice include a Higher Education Academy subject centre or an organisation such as the Staff and Educational Development Association (SEDA). An example of a more informal community of practice is a cross-institutional network, for example the Forum for the Enhancement of Learning and Teaching (FELT) whose membership is drawn from the universities of Dundee, St Andrews and Abertay, Dundee, in Scotland. The collaborative culture that supports the establishment and maintenance of communities of practice, and effective networking, also forms a central element of our next area for discussion – team working.

TEAM WORKING

Collaborating as a member of a team means working closely with colleagues who will be relying on you to fulfil a particular role, and to carry out that role both appropriately and effectively, in a group-working situation. The following checklist (adapted from Baldwin and Austin, 1995, cited in Paulsen and Feldman, 1995) suggests characteristics that good collaborators should bring to a team:

- some prior knowledge of your potential collaborators (gained either from working with them previously, speaking with other colleagues, or checking out their profiles from your institutional website);

- a clear idea of what you bring to the team in terms of knowledge, communications skills, values, ideas, etc.;
- preparedness to renegotiate team roles and responsibilities as appropriate;
- the ability to work as a team player and to establish positive working relationships with the other team members;
- the confidence to clarify and discuss with others your understanding of the team and the tasks it has to undertake (particularly in relation to timescale, allocation of roles and responsibilities, etc.).

The attributes of being a good team member are very similar to those required for students undertaking effective group work. Jaques (2000) identifies these attributes as including critical thinking, understanding, personal growth, communication skills and self-direction in learning. Working in a team with other colleagues provides you with an opportunity to model these qualities for your students!

Team teaching is the result of colleagues working together to develop, produce and deliver teaching. Working together in this way can produce many benefits both for staff and students, including: a more clearly articulated and supported course rationale or philosophy; increased coherence and better alignment between teaching methodologies and student assessment; and greater understanding of the way in which the course or module operates. Effective team teaching comprises:

- shared ownership of resources – contributing to and jointly producing teaching materials;
- keeping everyone involved – communicating regularly, not just in scheduled meetings, with all members of the team;
- providing feedback and support to all members of the team;
- maintaining a unified front in the classroom (development and changes take place as a result of feedback, review and discussion, not through 'front of house' arguments!);
- modelling effective team-working for colleagues and students;
- sharing learning through resources, experience and opportunities.

(Adapted from Brown and Race, 1995)

Furthermore, team teaching can help us on a personal level in a number of ways, such as developing teaching skills through experiential learning and providing opportunities for peer evaluation and observation of practice. Such opportunities can extend to coaching or informal development of new skills, more considered lesson planning, and intellectual stimulation – bouncing ideas off one another or perhaps carrying out collaborative research into your teaching practice. Becoming part of a team is not always easy, however, particularly for academics who have spent many years shut away on their own as researchers. In Case study 6.2, one of us shares our initial experiences of team teaching.

Case study 6.2
LEARNING TO BECOME A TEAM PLAYER

Coming from a background of mainly research, with limited teaching experience under my belt, I discovered that team teaching was a very different world. Previously, I had been left pretty much to my own devices in terms of planning and organising my teaching, but a new job role took me out of that situation and I became part of a teaching team.

At team meetings we would sit around the table and try to plan the curriculum for the coming academic year, but the meetings tended to deteriorate very quickly into shouting matches between myself and other colleagues, as we had quite different views on how the material should be delivered. My attempts to discuss the issues only seemed to raise the temperature further as they considered themselves to be 'right' and that I was 'wrong'. And I suppose I felt the opposite. This situation carried on for some time and, despite my colleagues and I having a good working relationship outside the meeting room, we made little progress within it.

I began to discuss the situation with another colleague from the team who I noticed never took part in our arguments and always seemed to maintain a cool head. How did she do it? As we began to work more closely together, I began to realise and value the benefits of colleagues who could help me to look at myself and my work more critically. Over the months I became less defensive about my work and more open to discussing alternatives. I came to realise that challenges to my ideas were not threats to my academic credibility but were opportunities for me to become more objective and critical and to learn the skills of self-evaluation. In team meetings I learned to listen more, feel less threatened by criticism and become more open to the ideas of my colleagues.

It is centrally important to working together effectively that everyone involved in the team is regarded as a real member of that team; this should include graduate tutors and support staff, who may normally only be included at the end stages of team planning in order to run tutorials, pick up routine assessment or record student marks. Failure to involve everyone, as appropriate, in the team as a whole can lead to confusion and misunderstanding of course requirements, poor alignment of teaching and assessment approaches, and a lack of confidence in the course from both staff and students. Anne Thorne in Case study 6.3 demonstrates the variety of partnerships that can be created through working with others, and the importance of keeping everyone involved 'in the loop'.

Case study 6.3
A LOT TO OFFER

Universities cannot go it alone. Or rather, for maximum effectiveness and flexibility, collaborative working has a lot to offer. I have come to this conclusion after being involved in a collaborative partnership between my university, employers and students that provided a genuine 'value added' aspect to joint working.

A need to build up a business ethic and attract more postgraduate students led us into partnership with a number of external organisations. This situation was further developed and validated by requests from previous students, now gainfully employed, to engage with them in their workplaces. This communication led to a turnaround within our institution. From a situation where we were failing to match student qualifications with the needs of employers, and where we needed to change our style of working in order to secure business, we began to customise our approach and to win tenders against other leading competitors.

In order to achieve this we began to work with our students and their prospective employers as opposed to second-guessing their requirements. We developed a more student-focused curriculum, which included new methods of delivery, the establishment of learning contracts and the setting-up of action learning sets. Essentially, we tailored our curriculum to meet student and employer demands, leading to benefits all round. We were no longer just selling a service or providing a qualification but gaining valuable input to the curriculum and enhancing our teaching practice through 360 degree feedback. The link to organisational development supported the cyclical process of theory into practice and practice creating theory.

Collaborative working is not without its challenges. It is essential to allow adequate time to prepare and to spend time on a consultation period. Everyone also needs to be clear about both what they would like to achieve and what is realistic for them to achieve from the partnership. However, the benefits to teaching development, design and practice are many, and for us, working with and learning from others led to an enhanced learning experience that created synergies between the university, external organisations and students.

Ann Thorne, Faculty of Business and Law, Liverpool John Moores University

TABLE 6.3 Models of team teaching

Team model	Features	Level of collaboration
Star	Loosely constructed team where one individual has overall control of course design but is joined by guest lecturers at the delivery stage.	Low levels of collaboration
Hierarchical	More consolidated team where one individual has overall control of course design but other team members play specific roles within course delivery.	Low to medium levels of collaboration
Specialist	Fully integrated team where individuals play a role in course design and delivery that relates to their specialisms. More than one team member normally present at all teaching sessions.	High levels of collaboration
Generalist	Fully integrated team where all individuals play a role in design and delivery and can take on the roles of others as required. More than one team member normally present at all teaching sessions.	Very high levels of collaboration
Interactive	A very small team, of only two or three members, who jointly design and deliver the course. Teaching roles are not prescribed and the classroom experience remains fluid in response to teacher–student interactions.	Exceptionally high levels of collaboration

Source: Adapted from Easterby-Smith and Olve, 1984, cited in Paulson and Feldman, 1995.

There are a number of different kinds of teams in which you may find yourself, however, not all of which will adhere to the suggested features for effective team working as noted above. Think about some of the teams in which you are involved and compare their organisation and ways of working with the models identified in Table 6.3.

The organisation, structure and purpose of a team can be adapted to address different situations. It is important, however, that the members of the team all have a clear understanding of what kind of team they are in, what their role is within the team and the purpose of the team's collaborative activity. In Case study 6.4, Povl Götke and his colleagues demonstrate the steps they have taken to create a specialist team in order better to support their students' learning.

Case study 6.4
DEVELOPING THE SPECIALIST TEAM

Unplanned, unstructured and random team teaching can be the result of an ad hoc getting together of like-minded colleagues. We have tried another approach, however, where we have put together a team built upon a range of different strengths and backgrounds. With an academic leading the curriculum development and two librarians with responsibility for the e-learning platform and electronic information searching, we set up our new programme.

Students were organised into small groups and were assigned a task to be solved where they had to address a number of requirements – for example, everyone had to include at least three articles in their answer and to organise their co-operative working via an e-learning platform. What was important here was that all the groups received support and advice from a subject specialist. Librarians advised on the task of searching for information and articles, and guidance with e-learning enabled the collaborative development of a specialised professional database where working papers, notes, links and references could be deposited.

The advantage of taking this approach to teaching is that every single member of the team provides a valuable, specialised contribution to the overall picture. It provides a more organic and unified structure to team teaching, which is also challenging and rewarding, where individuals cannot avoid relating to, reflecting on, discussing and developing the team itself in support of student learning.

TABLE 6.4 Life stages of the team

Group life stage	Features
Forming	The team is created
Storming	The team go through a period of adjustment and getting to know one another
Norming	Group cohesion is created; conflict is reconciled and mutual support develops
Performing	Constructive team working develops
Mourning	The group dissolves

Source: Based on Tuckman, 1965.

Undoubtedly the bringing together of individuals within the team who represented the educational and instructional side of things, combined with the information retrieval and e-learning skills of the librarians, was a great advantage to the successful development of such a programme. While these individuals, and the sections of the academic community that they represent, are traditionally closely related, the structured integration provided by the team demonstrated the strength of a multidisciplinary approach in supporting student learning.

Povl Götke, Jens Dam and Gina Bay, Teaching and Learning, University of Southern Denmark

Becoming part of a team means participating in the life stages of that team, in addition to carrying out the tasks for which that team was set up. These life stages normally follow a predictable pattern of forming, storming, norming, performing and mourning, as identified in Table 6.4.

The end of a period of collaborative working is a time for review and reflection. Consider what you have learned, what you can take forward to your next experience with team teaching and the ways in which you can continue to include collaborative working within your own practice in order to develop your teaching.

CONCLUSION

Working with others has a lot to offer in terms of developing your teaching. Who can you work with? Colleagues, mentors, a buddy group, staff developers – the possibilities are only curtailed by the limitations of your personal networks. Look out for projects, funding opportunities, interdisciplinary work and other collaborative ways of working. Consider putting the following suggestions into practice in order to begin actively and effectively to work with others in developing your teaching:

- Clarify what you want to achieve from collaborative working.
- Do not wait to be asked – approach colleagues yourself.
- Find common ground and establish a rapport with colleagues with whom you would like to work.
- Discuss with them potential ways in which collaborative working could support *your* development.
- Discuss with them potential ways in which collaborative working could support *their* development.
- Suggest ways of taking collaborative working forward.

(Adapted from Warren and Gielnik, 1995)

REFERENCES

Baldwin, R. G. and Austin, A. E. (1995) 'Faculty Collaboration in Teaching', in Seldin, P. (ed.), *Improving College Teaching*. Boston, MA: Anker.

Brown, S. and Race, P. (1995) *Assess Your Own Teaching Quality*. London: Kogan Page.

Campbell, A., McNamara, O. and Gilroy, P. (2004) *Practitioner Research and Professional Development in Education*. London: Paul Chapman.

Easterby-Smith, M. and Olve, N. (1984). 'Team Teaching: Making Management Education More Student Centred?'. *Management Education and Development*, 15, 3, 221–36.

Higher Education Academy subject centres. Online, accessed 24 September 2005, www.heacademy.ac.uk/474.htm.

Jaques, D. (2000) *Learning in Groups*, third edition. London: Kogan Page.

Paulsen, M. and Feldman, K. (1995) *Taking Teaching Seriously: Meeting the Challenge of Instructional Improvement*. ASHE-ERIC Higher Education Report No. 2. Washington, DC: The George Washington University.

Staff and Educational Development Association (SEDA). Online, accessed 24 September 2005, www.seda.ac.uk.

Trowler, P. and Knight, P. (2000) 'Coming to Know in Higher Education', in Tight, M. (ed.) (2004) *The RoutledgeFalmer Reader in Higher Education*. London: RoutledgeFalmer.

Tuckman, B. W. (1965) 'Developmental Sequences in Small Groups'. *Psychological Bulletin*, 63, 384–99.

Warren, E. and Gielnik, C. (1995) *Empower Yourself: Self Development for Women*. London: The Industrial Society.

Wenger, E., McDermott, R. and Snyder, W. (2002) *Cultivating Communities of Practice*. Boston, MA: Harvard Business School Press.

FURTHER READING

Kenway, J., Epstein, D. and Boden, R. (2005) *Building Networks*. London: Sage.

Chapter 7

Mentoring

> Mentoring is essentially an interpersonal process . . . big ears, small mouth . . .
>
> (Gibbons, undated)

INTRODUCTION

Mentoring is very much in vogue. Programmes and projects are everywhere, promoting the view that in order to get ahead, further your professional development and progress in your career, a mentor is invaluable. But what can you expect from mentoring in terms of developing your teaching? Essentially, a mentoring relationship is centred on learning. Starting out in a new job role, taking on a new challenge, or moving into a different phase of your career are all aspects of your practice where mentoring can have a role to play. However, it is important to be realistic. Having a mentor will not automatically make you a better teacher – you will have to be prepared to share issues with your mentor, discuss ideas and strategies, reflect on your own development and be prepared to make your own decisions. It is not the mentor's job to do this for you but instead to support you in achieving your objectives.

This chapter considers the role that mentoring can play in helping you to develop your teaching and highlights aspects of mentoring in action, including working with your mentor as a role model, supporter and critical friend. We also discuss the potential tensions that can arise within mentoring relationships and suggest ways in which these situations can be defused and reconstructed as positive learning opportunities.

DEVELOPING YOUR TEACHING THROUGH MENTORING

The original 'mentor' was a wise and trusted counsellor or adviser from Greek mythology, but mentoring is a term now used to describe a developmental relationship between colleagues, one of whom will (normally) be a more experienced practitioner. Mentoring relationships facilitate personal and professional development through support, challenge and review and have real potential to help us in developing our teaching as the primary focus is on learning and growth.

The following attributes have all been associated with mentors: coach, adviser, advocate, supporter, role model, motivator, counsellor, critical friend, challenger, and facilitator – making a mentor sound almost superhuman! Undeniably, mentors carry out a multi-skilled role. This can involve:

- listening to concerns
- identifying problems
- modelling appropriate behaviour
- confronting negativity
- challenging views and actions
- reviewing current practice
- helping to consolidate learning,

and potentially many other things, depending on the nature of each specific mentoring relationship.

From the specific viewpoint of using mentoring in order to develop your teaching, in this chapter we plan to look at three of these aspects in greater detail as identified in Figure 7.1: mentor as role model, supporter and critical friend.

DEVELOPING YOUR TEACHING: MENTOR AS ROLE MODEL

Seeking good role models for our teaching practice is an important step in helping us to develop as the kind of teacher we want to be. The idea of looking at others in order to discover who we are may seem contradictory at first, but let us think about it. How do we begin as teachers? We tend to develop a style based on the teaching that we ourselves have experienced. This may mean emulating that great school

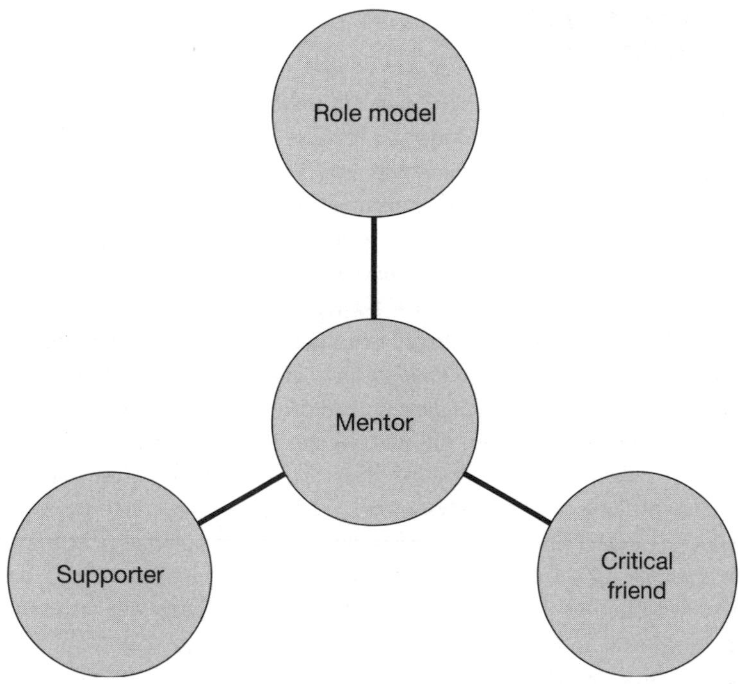

FIGURE 7.1 The multi-faceted role of the mentor

teacher who inspired us to enter our particular discipline or the lecturer who made classes lively and interesting – or it could mean avoiding the methods of those teachers who failed to inspire us. This approach can provide a sound starter kit of teaching approaches and strategies but it is also self-limiting. The challenge for us now is to develop a teaching style that works for our students; a potentially much more diverse group of individuals with a variety of learning styles and approaches to learning.

Engaging with colleagues and seeking out those positive role models will support you in developing your own individual teaching style and repertoire. Working with a mentor will give you the added bonus of a closer, more structured relationship with defined goals and targets within which you can interrogate, challenge and debate aspects of practice. In Case study 7.1, Wafa Nicholls describes the long-lasting impact, particularly in relation to role modelling, that two informal 'mentors' have had on his teaching practice.

Case study 7.1
FLYING SOLO

I began my teaching career 'flying solo' in the lecture theatre without the benefit of an 'introduction to teaching' course, which is now available to new lecturers in my institution. I was very fortunate, however, in being supported through my early experiences of teaching by two exceptional colleagues. Although no formal mentorship programme existed, they were to me true mentors, whose guidance and enthusiasm not only helped me to find my feet in teaching but still shape my approach to teaching today.

They provided me with wonderful role models: highlighting the importance of continuing professional development in teaching and learning through their attendance at staff development workshops; introducing me to the concept of reflective teaching; and guiding me through what seemed to be a maze of unfamiliar administrative rules and regulations. Most importantly, they left me with two timeless pieces of advice: document your teaching practice (for example in a teaching portfolio); and never be afraid to acknowledge that you do not know the answer to a student's question. This is an important part of the unwritten curriculum, and while honesty will not result in a loss of face, attempting to bluff it out will!

I still value the advice that I received from my unofficial mentors and I try to emulate them by offering my support to new colleagues. Not only has pursuing the new role of mentor given me the personal satisfaction of helping others, it has also had a positive and, for me, unexpected effect on my teaching. Explaining to mentees how I approach various teaching tasks, and answering questions about why I have not used an alternative method, has forced me to review and where necessary reassess those teaching habits that have become routine over the years. The result has been that I have found myself guided to a deeper level of reflective teaching than I have ever experienced previously. The benefits of a good mentor can stay with you for the rest of your teaching career.

Wafa Nicholls, Genetics, King Abdul Aziz University

DEVELOPING YOUR TEACHING: MENTOR AS SUPPORTER

We all need to feel supported in the decisions that we make and the actions that we take. Case study 7.2, based on the experiences of one of us as a relatively new lecturer in a new job, discusses the role that an informal mentor can have in supporting our learning and development.

Case study 7.2
MY FIRST MENTOR

I changed horses mid-race, if you like, moving from one discipline to another as one career door closed and another opened. It was exciting moving into a new area but also very challenging. At times the learning curve was so steep it felt as if it was vertical. It was a new world, with a more senior role, and a new 'language'. However, I was really fortunate in that one of my new colleagues was incredibly supportive and encouraging. She helped me to find my feet and my confidence in the new area. What did she do that was so helpful? It is hard to put into words, really. She was supportive, encouraging and never patronising. We talked a lot – about all sorts of things. We planned teaching sessions together, she gave me ideas and also helped me to think about my own. As my mentor she played a number of roles – supporting me but also quietly questioning some of my more strident views, challenging them and getting me to look at them more critically. I wanted to have her vision and foresight and she became my role model for developing as a teacher in my new discipline. We have also become good friends, but we still have that ability to step outside ourselves and to become more objective and evaluate what the other is doing. I suppose, although I did not think about this until later, that she was my first mentor. It was extremely valuable for me and I owe her a lot.

This example centred around an informal mentoring relationship. Many universities, however, have formal mentoring schemes, and perhaps the most common use of such schemes is in probationary mentoring, as part of the induction or probationary process for new staff, where a more senior colleague is appointed to work with the new appointee over a specific period of time. This form of mentoring can be described as following the apprenticeship model – where the mentor is a senior colleague whose role is to act as 'master craftsman' and to provide learning opportunities. Other models of mentoring include:

- peer development model – both individuals in the relationship are of equal status and development is collaborative;
- co-mentoring model – group mentoring in a non-hierarchical relationship based on reciprocity.

Table 7.1 highlights the stages at which each type of mentoring is most commonly found or most readily available.

TABLE 7.1 Models of mentoring

Career phase	Model of mentoring	Feature
Novice teacher	Apprenticeship model	Formal mentoring where the mentor is usually allocated
Continuing professional development in teaching	Peer development model	Informal mentoring where the mentor is usually self-selected
Sharing practice as a more experienced teacher	Co-mentoring model	Peer mentoring or becoming a mentor yourself

Source: Adapted from Nicholls, 2002.

Regardless of the kind of mentoring relationship you are in, one of the central roles for your mentor is to support you in discovering more about yourself in terms of your potential, skills and abilities, and the ways in which this self-knowledge can be used to support you in developing your teaching. One of the ways in which this can be achieved is through the identification, creation or support of learning opportunities. Think about what would constitute opportunities for you under each of the headings listed in Table 7.2.

Supported learning is an excellent way to enable you to develop your teaching. Nonetheless, unremitting support is of less value than support with challenge, where your mentor will help you in critiquing

TABLE 7.2 Learning opportunities available through mentoring

Opportunities to . . .	Example in action . . .
Gain exposure to new learning	Workplace shadow your mentor
Use and reinforce new learning	Team teach with your mentor
Accelerate learning	Discuss and debate issues with your mentor; put them into practice; follow up with review and reflection
Reflect upon learning	Engage in Socratic dialogue with your mentor

Source: Adapted from Zachary, 2000.

and illuminating issues and proposals, before supporting you in their implementation, by carrying out the role of a critical friend.

DEVELOPING YOUR TEACHING: MENTOR AS CRITICAL FRIEND

Having supportive colleagues makes for a very positive workplace in which to experiment with and develop your teaching practice. There is nothing more deflating than a work environment where the ethos of 'that's the way we've always done things around here' holds sway, accompanied by a pressure not to rock the boat with new ideas and approaches. Nonetheless, support without challenge provides only half the value. A mentor can play the part of a critical friend who, while supporting your ideas, will also be able to draw attention to any weaker areas, and then go on to review those with you. This process provides a continuous cycle of supported and critical evaluation that can lead to enhanced practice.

How does a critical friendship work in practice? For MacDonald (1986, cited in Campbell *et al.*, 2004: 108) adopting the role of the critical friend 'gives teachers the power to determine their own agenda and to explore the role of theory in their teaching lives and may let them be in charge of the "knowledge-creation process" instead of having the ideas of others imposed'. There is a strong focus on confrontation, questioning and review, deconstruction, reconstruction and development of practice. In other words, it is hard graft! But it is all the more valuable for it, and all the more value-added when working with a mentor in their role as a critical friend as a result of the opportunities for feedback, evaluation and triangulation. As with all aspects of the mentoring relationship, it may be useful to discuss with your mentor their role as a critical friend and how you anticipate it working within your relationship. You might like also to introduce theoretical models to support your discussion, such as Egan's (1990) skilled helper model (cited in Campbell *et al.*, 2004), shown in Table 7.3.

Consider extending the value of the critical friend by working with an action learning set. These are essentially groups of critical friends who meet together to discuss and consider a particular issue or concern. At each meeting, one individual has the chance to have his or her issue examined and discussed in detail within the action learning set. As with mentoring, the role of the set is not to offer advice immediately or to tell the individual what they should do, but rather to explore the issue

TABLE 7.3 **Egan's skilled helper model applied to the role of critical friend**

- Explore issues through open-ended questions that focus on the experience of the mentee
- Focus on a specific aspect as identified by the mentee
- Consider new perspectives on the issue through appropriate questioning
- Move forward through action planning with the mentee
- Establish realistic goals with the mentee
- Monitor and reflect on progress through the use of an evaluation cycle of 'plan, do and review'
- Develop and use criteria with which to evaluate the level of achievement or learning

Source: Based on Egan, 1990.

in greater depth by open questioning, providing support and challenge throughout, and by allowing the individual concerned to arrive at their own, informed, decisions. Essentially, the action learning set is a form of group mentoring. In Case study 7.3, Stuart Mackay discusses the value that he has gained from involvement in an action learning set.

Case study 7.3
SEE THE WORLD AS OTHERS SEE IT

I took part in an action learning set for a period of three years. This involved meeting with a group of seven people once a fortnight to support each other as we each undertook a project related to both our work and an educational qualification. Being together with the same people over a long period of time built up trust and familiarity and produced a very supportive and nurturing environment. Working on a work-related project meant that we often brought issues to the set that were familiar problems to us all.

Over time we were able to communicate very effectively and share our underpinning emotions. Emerging from this experience was a fantastic opportunity to 'see the world as others see it'. This led to the insight that actually I was not really that different to many of my colleagues! We often experienced the same powerful motivating forces such as fear of failure, not wanting to make a fool of oneself, anxiety and fatigue. Such factors have a powerful moderating effect on the way we behave and hence the way we appear to others. This realisation enabled me to feel closer to other teachers and learners and to understand others' behaviour more. I became more tolerant of others and looked to see how they might be seeing the world. For example, I observed a colleague chairing a meeting poorly. Instead of feeling angry or that this meeting was a waste of my time, I soon realised it was because they were feeling anxious about their performance as chair. I worked on trying to reduce the individual's anxiety by pointing out the positive aspects of their chairing technique so that next time they might feel less anxious and perform better. This key learning point helped me to understand and work with my colleagues in a more effective way.

So I believe one of the most important ways of developing my practice is to try and get to know people as individuals and realise that we all have very similar motivating forces to our behaviour. Trying to 'see the world as others see it' helps to keep me rooted in a reality shared with other teachers and learners.

Stuart Mackay, Directorate of Radiography, Salford University

While many aspects of mentoring are wholly positive, the interpersonal and intense nature of the relationship can also create issues and tensions. In this next section we explore some of the common challenges found in mentoring relationships.

WORKING WITH CHALLENGES IN MENTORING

Some mentoring relationship can create unexpected issues or tensions. Mentoring schemes aim to match mentors and mentees sensitively but this is not always possible when the individuals are not well known to the organisers of the scheme. Choosing your own mentor can also have pitfalls. Personality clashes can emerge in even the most sociable of colleagues when they are placed in a new and different relationship. This is a situation that can work very well, but you both need to be absolutely clear about when you are wearing the 'different hats' of friend/colleague and mentor/mentee, even down to the point of actually stating that you are now putting a different hat on – or taking it off! If you want, or are in a position, to select your own mentor, you might like to think about how your potential choice matches up against the following skills and values identified in effective mentors (adapted from Whittaker and Cartwright, 2000):

- genuinely interested in mentoring as a professional development approach;
- willing to give their time to others;
- good communicator and a good listener;
- positive but realistic viewpoint;
- non-judgemental in their approach;
- prepared to provide challenge and constructive criticism.

Regardless of the level of formality of the mentoring in which you are involved, it is worth establishing clear aims and perhaps negotiating basic ground rules at the beginning of the relationship. These ground rules can be reviewed as necessary in order to ensure that the relationship is continuing to serve its purpose. Topics for ground rules that you might want to consider include:

- How often, where and for how long will we meet?
- How formally? Will a minute be kept of the meetings? Who will take the minute? (And who will have access to it?)
- Will discussions during our relationship be confidential?
- What are the aims and/or goals of the relationship and what criteria will be used to measure their success?
- What are the roles and responsibilities of the mentor and the mentee?
- How long will the mentoring relationship last?

Let us consider these points in turn.

■ It is important to discuss at an early stage how often you will meet as you and your mentor may have very different expectations! The regularity of the meetings will depend on the overall length of the proposed mentoring relationship and the other forms of contact and support that your mentor is willing to engage in, e.g. email, telephone, video conferencing. Are there other kinds of activities, apart from meetings, in which you would like to involve your mentor? Will you want your mentor to observe your teaching practice and provide feedback?

Do you anticipate that your mentor will be available to double-mark assessments? Remember that although your mentor may start off as a colleague in your department, research trips, sabbaticals or a change of job may mean that regular face-to-face contact is no longer possible or becomes difficult. If you want to continue that particular relationship, then you will need to consider an alternative form of contact with which both you and your mentor are happy.

- Similarly, give some thought as to how long your meetings will be. This may vary over the duration of the relationship, and it is worthwhile to discuss the amount of time that you both have available at the beginning of every meeting. This will avoid anxious clock-watching for both of you.

- Deciding on where you will hold the meetings is very important. The best solution is to choose neutral territory but try to avoid public spaces, such as staff coffee-rooms, in order to avoid having to carry out what may be a confidential discussion *sotto voce*. A meeting room or small teaching room is useful. Remember to stick a notice on the door to indicate that you are having a meeting and to avoid interruptions.

- Make sure that both you and your mentor are clear – and comfortable – about whether a minute of the meeting will be kept. If one is to be kept, are you clear about its purpose – formal requirement, personal aide-memoire, 'to do' list? Where will it be kept and who else might have access to it? Even if your immediate reaction to this suggestion is negative, do not dismiss the idea out of hand. Reflect on why it might be useful for you to keep a record of your meetings. It could provide part of a 'paper trail' of your development as a teacher that you could include in a teaching portfolio. Or it could provide a personal record of your development that you could use for private reflection or for appraisal or review purposes.

- In 'pure' forms of mentoring, the relationship is a confidential one. However, not all mentoring relationships will take this form. Some may contain elements of supervision and links to review or appraisal, where confidentiality may not be possible, while others might be an informal part of a teaching team's development, where confidentiality may be seen as unnecessary. The most important aspect of confidentiality in relation to your mentoring relationship is clarifying and agreeing on what aspects, if any, of your discussions will be confidential.

■ Having a realistic end point for the mentoring relationship is also important. Some relationships – such as the achievement of a particular goal or project – have a natural ending. This may not be quite so clear for other mentoring situations and it is worthwhile discussing this aspect at the outset of the relationship.

In Case study 7.4 Jane Hibberd explains that while it took time for her to settle into her mentoring relationship it was well worth it in the end.

Case study 7.4
MAKING MENTORING WORK FOR ME

I feel privileged to have a mentor, especially one specifically to guide me throughout my probationary period. I have had previous experience in being mentored – while working in clinical practice as an occupational therapist. However, the main difference this time round – while undertaking the Postgraduate Certificate in Higher Education Practice (PGCHEP) – is that whereas previously I chose my mentor, this time I had one allocated to me. Perhaps this was not such a bad idea as I was new to my current role as tutor in occupational therapy, and I was not aware of who might have had gaps in their workloads that would allow them to take on the role of mentor. The first mentor–mentee meeting occurred within ten days of my initial employment date – not bad at all!

I feel that in order for a mentoring relationship to work well, it is important to find out what makes the other person 'tick'. My relationship with my mentor took time to establish as she was quite disciplined in her approach. However, once we began to settle into the relationship, and to find out things about one another, it began to work for me. I discovered that my mentor likes to knuckle down to the task immediately when we meet, so I began to take the same approach and found that this produced results swiftly. My mentor set specific targets for me, and this has enabled me to complete my personal development plan. Meanwhile, I like to take responsibility for leading the mentoring meetings and aim to be well prepared for our sessions, outlining the issues or concerns that I would like to discuss in the form of a checklist.

Reflecting back on this, I realise that because of my mentor's approach, I am now ahead of my colleagues who started their studies on the PGCHEP at the same time as me.

Jane Hibberd, School of Allied Health Professions, University of East Anglia

You may find yourself in a number of different kinds of mentoring relationships at different times in your career. We now take a look at three potential scenarios and discuss ways of making mentoring work in each of these situations.

As a new lecturer you may be allocated a mentor under a mentoring scheme for new members of staff. The majority of new teaching staff normally undergo a period of 'probation', following which they will be confirmed in post (if they meet the requirements of probation). This system can work well in that your new mentor can 'show you the ropes' and help you to settle into your new job in addition to supporting your overall development as a teacher. The success of this form of mentoring does depend, however, on the extent to which your appointed mentor is committed to the process, their previous experiences of mentoring and the time available for them to carry out the role.

Probationary mentors should be carefully matched to individuals, but this is not always the case. There may also be an implicit management or supervisory role, beyond support and guidance, within this kind of mentoring, which adds a different dimension to the relationship. This can result in you feeling reluctant to discuss aspects of your practice that you find difficult or challenging, as your mentor may also be assessing your overall performance in addition to supporting your development. Consider the following example shown in Box 7.1, where a new member of staff is struggling to build up a relationship with her mentor.

Mentoring in a probationary situation, where feedback from the mentor can have a significant impact on whether an individual is confirmed in post, can be stressful for mentors as well as the probationary lecturer. There are a number of steps that you can take, however, to make this form of mentoring a positive experience:

- Begin by familiarising yourself with the relevant institutional guidelines concerning mentoring for new lecturers, including the aims and objectives of the scheme.

Box 7.1
THE PROBATIONARY MENTOR

My mentor is pulling me in two directions. He is my Head of Department, and on the one hand I'm glad that he is giving me his time and I'm really learning from his expertise, but on the other hand I'm reluctant to discuss my issues or questions with him in case he thinks I'm incompetent and not up to working in his department. We seem to get on well when we're chatting in the coffee room but I can't relax and feel comfortable with him in our mentoring meetings – particularly as he takes lots of notes and I don't know what he's writing! – so I just tend to listen and not ask too many questions.

- Think about these aspects and how they might relate to your personal development goals, then raise and discuss them with your mentor.
- Aim to build a positive relationship with your mentor, and be confident and clear in expressing your ideas on how you view the relationship.
- If you (or your mentor) feel uncertain about what should happen within mentoring, make enquiries about possible training opportunities. Mentors are usually busy and experienced colleagues. They may be unaware of the availability of training for mentoring or feel that their years of experience have provided them with sufficient 'on-the-job' experience. If you approach the idea of training from your side of the equation, suggesting that you would be interested in this opportunity (rather than implying that they need to take advantage of it!), then you may be more successful.
- And finally, be aware of what steps you can take if the relationship is not working.

Perhaps you need to learn a new technique or are entering a new field of specialism and are appointed a mentor. A possible concern is that your mentor may approach the relationship from a deficit rather than a developmental model, viewing their appointment as a response to your lack of skills rather than as a positive opportunity for personal and

Box 7.2
THE DEFICIT MODEL APPROACH TO MENTORING

I feel that my mentor thinks I'm stupid. She has been appointed to work with me in developing my course for online delivery as she's got a lot of experience in working with virtual learning environments. She's much younger than me, and not nearly as experienced in terms of teaching, but she talks to me as if I am a child. I know I've got a lot to learn in this area but I've also got years of experience of working with students. I think she spends so much time interacting online that she's forgotten how to communicate face to face.

professional development. A further consideration is that your mentor might not be the willing partner that you had anticipated. Ideally, he or she will have had time released from their normal workloads in which to engage in mentoring, but this is not always the case and you might be seen more as a burden than a joy. The example in Box 7.2 illustrates such a situation.

Clarification of the nature of this kind of mentoring is key to making this type of relationship work:

- Make anticipated time commitments explicit and outline your goals or targets for development with your mentor at the outset.
- Identify the existing skills that you already have on which you can build to develop in this area, and aim to work towards more collaborative learning.
- Identify an area of your expertise that could be helpful to your colleague, and suggest or work towards turning the situation into a peer mentoring relationship.

Your mentor should draw out your potential through confidence building, encouragement and by providing opportunities for you to demonstrate your learning. However, some individuals may see their appointment as mentor as little more than a showcase for their skills and abilities, as demonstrated in Box 7.3.

Box 7.3
THE DOMINANT MENTOR

I thought mentoring would be about my learning but all I seem to have developed into is an audience. My mentor and I work together in the same lab, and he is beginning to turn everything he does into an elaborate demonstration 'for my benefit'. Our other colleagues thought this was amusing at first, but now they are beginning to resent his constant pontificating – and so am I. I want to talk about my plans and discuss my questions, but all I hear about is how he does things, and the prizes he has won, and the books he has written. I don't think he's listening at all.

You can help to avoid this situation developing by discussing and clarifying the roles and responsibilities of 'mentor' and 'mentee' with your mentor from the beginning of your relationship:

- Be prepared to revisit these as often as required.
- Draw up a development plan that clearly identifies your goals and targets, and then review this plan with your mentor on a regular basis.
- Beware of alienating your mentor; listen to what they have to say and then discuss how you might adopt some of their ideas in your practice. Or after a demonstration of their expertise ask questions about their technique, but couch it in terms related to your own practice.

Adopting these strategies can help you to maintain the focus on (your) learning as opposed to (your mentor's) teaching.

CONCLUSION

Mentoring can have a significant impact on your development as a teacher, but it is not without its challenges and potential pitfalls. Having a mentor should not be viewed as a substitute for you actively aiming to develop and enhance your practice. Your mentor can provide a role model, a sounding board for ideas and proposals, and a supporter of your plans and actions, but only as the result of positive engagement and action on your part.

If you are not yet working with a mentor, think about the avenues that are open to you to pursue either informal or formal mentoring. If you are currently working with a mentor, consider the extent to which you have been able to grow in the following areas of your practice and reflect on the extent to which mentoring has supported you:

- development of enhanced interpersonal skills with students and colleagues;
- insight into your own teaching performance;
- increased ability to exploit learning opportunities;
- heightened sense of self-worth and confidence as a teacher;
- increased understanding of teaching and learning;
- exploration of your hidden potential in a particular aspect of your teaching practice;
- ability to set and achieve targets;
- gaining a new perspective on your teaching practice;
- satisfaction and stimulation through professional working with colleagues.

REFERENCES

Campbell, A., McNamara, O. and Gilroy, P. (2004) *Practitioner Research and Professional Development in Education*. London: Paul Chapman.

Egan, G. (1990) *The Skilled Helper: A Systematic Approach to Effective Helping*, fourth edition. Pacific Grove, CA: Brooks/Cole.

Gibbons, A. (undated) *The Coaching & Mentoring Network*. Online accessed 25 September 2005, www.coachingnetwork.org.uk.

MacDonald, J. (1986) 'Raising the Teacher's Voice and the Ironic Role of Theory', *Harvard Educational Review*, 56: 355–78.

Nicholls, G. (2002) 'Mentoring', in Peter Jarvis (ed.) *The Theory and Practice of Teaching*. London: Kogan Page.

Whittaker, M. and Cartwright, A. (2000) *The Mentoring Manual*. Aldershot: Gower.

Zachary, L. (2000) *The Mentor's Guide: Facilitating Effective Learning Relationships*. San Francisco, CA: Jossey-Bass.

FURTHER READING

Barnes, T. and Stiasny, M. (eds) (1995) *Mentoring: Making it Work*. Southampton: Bassett Press.

Fullerton, H. (ed.) (1996) *Facets of Mentoring in Higher Education 1*. Birmingham: SEDA.

Fullerton, H. (ed.) (1998) *Facets of Mentoring in Higher Education 2*. Birmingham: SEDA.

Segerman-Peck, L. (1991) *Networking & Mentoring: A Woman's Guide*. London: Piatkus.

Chapter 8

Development projects and research into learning

> 'Bluetooth' shouted one student, to much amusement from the others, and the silent game was over. She had created the arbitrary sentence 'they woke up to find a 500 foot crop circle' from tiny bits of paper and won the game that I'd invented to help explain issues around proximity, security, access privileges and 'pulling' information via mobile devices and Bluetooth technology.
>
> The activity was successful in making an otherwise very teacher-led session more student-focused. It enabled me to explore creativity in my teaching and I got a real sense of achievement out of seeing the students get so involved and having so much fun with a game I'd invented myself.
>
> (Nicola Foster, International Centre for Digital Content, Liverpool John Moores University)

INTRODUCTION: GAME OVER

The main reason why we develop our teaching is to improve student learning. We can see how introducing a development into our teaching will make a difference for our students, and so we get on with it – eventually breathing a sigh of relief once our 'game' is successfully over for the first time! The benefits may be felt not simply in the activity or new initiative itself but, as hinted at in the quote above, in a shift across our teaching more widely. It often takes something quite substantial to move the deep-seated attitudes that shape your practice.

This chapter aims to take you through the process of introducing a new development into your teaching. You might be significantly revising the way in which you teach an existing course unit, introducing a new one or experimenting with an innovative teaching method. We will draw on a variety of insights from the wider literature on project management as we consider such activity, while still addressing aspects of the development process that are more specific to education. Development projects can also provide the basis for more scholarly approaches, and we thus conclude the chapter by looking, more briefly, at how you might embark upon research into student learning.

THE DEVELOPMENT PROCESS

There is always a risk involved in trying something new. Will it work? Introducing a development takes you outside your comfort zone, almost by definition. At the very outset some confidence is required; you need to hold your nerve! There is a way in which you are entering into the unknown, a sense that Case study 8.1 by John Mitchell clearly captures. Confidence is, though, only an initial requirement: it helps to have an appreciation for the development process (see, for instance, Kahn and Baume, 2003). This forms a key element in your ability to carry a development through to its conclusion.

Case study 8.1
FUMBLING IN THE DARK

> They say that time changes things, but you actually have to change them yourself.
>
> Andy Warhol

Changing the way you teach always seems to require a certain leap of faith, even if you feel sure of the benefits. Introducing problem-based learning (PBL) in a traditional electronic engineering curriculum where this approach to learning is virtually unheard of therefore presented something of a challenge!

Designing a PBL module for the third-year curriculum felt like standing at the front door of an unfamiliar, darkened house. Not only was the layout unfamiliar but the final goal was still something of a mystery. My starting point was the academic literature, which encouraged me to venture further down the path but offered little in the way of guidance as to how to proceed. The only thing for it was to trust to luck and try to press on forward.

Slowly, very slowly at times, as my eyes became adjusted to the darkness, chinks of light started appearing; newfound colleagues with educational backgrounds who were willing to translate the literature from their field gave this engineer a torch, and students from pilot studies illuminated the terrain still further by suggesting that PBL is more interesting and helps them to engage.

The analogy is apt: from the spark needed to set you on the development process, to the shards of light shed by early trials, to the relief when light emerges, a radical curriculum development project can be an unnerving experience. Giving up the control you usually exercise in a traditional lecture room and setting your students on the same darkened path you have just trodden is difficult, and you can only hope they too find a torch. But when you open the door and see a class full of enthusiastic students working in groups, discussing the problem at hand, it is clear to see that the bruised shins from fumbling in the dark were worth the effort.

John Mitchell, Department of Electronic and Electrical Engineering,
University College London

DESIGNING AND IMPLEMENTING THE DEVELOPMENT

The development process involves an initial stage where you assess a range of considerations to give shape to your plans. There are plenty of things that you could do – the skill in developing education is to pick an initiative that has a realistic chance of making it. Four considerations are particularly significant:

- Setting a clear aim for your development – at the outset it is important to be clear what you are trying to achieve. What is the challenge for students or teachers that you are seeking to address?
- Understanding the needs of all those involved – this understanding will come in part from your own experience, but it may also draw on a more formal analysis of the needs, perhaps informed by student feedback or even focus groups.
- Awareness of the activity that others have already carried out – there is a growing body of case studies on development in higher education, as we have already seen in Chapter 2.

It clearly makes sense to carry out a review of the literature, perhaps following the model provided in Figure 2.1, and relevant practice before embarking on the design. This can include taking a look at relevant educational theory, to provide a framework to understand and shape the development, reducing reliance on trial and error. Drawing on this prior work more fully might well help to reduce your sense of uncertainty as you embark on something new.

- A rich vein of ideas on which to draw – this enables you to select the most promising ideas as a basis for the development, increasing your chances of success. Ideas do not appear from nowhere but are often triggered by exchanges with others (see Gustavsen, 2001). Networking, as explored in Chapter 6, is thus essential, as are more open exchanges with students.

The design of the development should respect such considerations, rather than simply be invented from scratch, otherwise you may well run into difficulty. For instance, if you simply jump in with a 'good idea', and immediately invent your teaching materials, you may find your development is irrelevant after all to your students' needs. This initial assessment of what is worth developing provides a clear basis for overall design of the development.

Addressing these considerations will help ensure that your development is fit for purpose, but a development project also involves introducing change into an existing environment, and it is thus important to take into account the factors that will support or hinder your new initiative when it comes to implementation. The idea itself may be an excellent one, but other factors will also determine whether it can be successfully implemented in practice. The complexity of higher education means that adaptations to your initial plans will often be required, and these need to be possible.

Table 8.1 analyses the forces that give leverage for change, whether within yourself, relating to your immediate working group, stemming from wider organisational issues or the broader higher education environment (see Roche, 2003). As far as small-scale development is concerned, the personal and social factors matter most, and as developments increase in scale, organisational and sector-wide issues clearly grow in importance.

On the personal level, which is where we focus most attention in Table 8.1, motivation is certainly essential, and is likely to be enhanced if you can use the development for more than one purpose. You might use a development project as a way to take forward your own teaching, and thus to enhance your students' educational experiences; but it could also count towards assessment on a programme in learning and teaching; you can use it to secure funding, to develop further expertise, as evidence for a promotion or to develop stronger relationships with colleagues. As far as ability and experience is concerned, for example, an ability to manage a project is essential, something we will explore in the next section.

We can also pick out from Table 8.1 the importance of collaboration with colleagues, an issue that Hilary Rollin explores in Case study 8.2. You will typically involve colleagues in actually delivering the project, and they need to be on board; perhaps approval needs to be secured for the project to go ahead, and when difficulties occur someone else may be better placed to provide a solution. It is particularly important to assess the likely contribution of your colleagues, given that they can either provide assistance at key points or create barriers to progress on the project.

Review point 8.1
SELECTING A DEVELOPMENT

Identify two developments that you might consider introducing into your teaching. Assess their relative merits against each of the factors outlined in Table 8.1.

Case study 8.2
ENGAGING COLLEAGUES IN A DEVELOPMENT

So you are all set to produce some brilliant new materials that colleagues will have to use? Excellent; but before you start thumping the keyboard in the wee small hours, take a step back. Try to recall how it felt when a colleague approached you in a state of euphoria with some hot-off-the-press materials, and all you had to do was deliver them to an enraptured class.

TABLE 8.1 Forces that support or hinder the success of development projects

Category of force	Force for change	Comment
Personal	Motivation	You need a genuine commitment to making the development happen, and to facing the difficulties that will arise on the way.
	Ability and experience	Projects will call on your ability to manage others, work to tight timescales, design educational materials, and so on.
	Resources	You need to be realistic, making sure that you have adequate time and resources to carry out the development, and to respond to challenges that are likely to arise.
Social	Collaboration	Collaboration helps to ensure that the development is rooted in the real world, and actually happens. This may also allow the scale of the development to grow. The extent to which suitable collaborators are available is thus a key factor in assessing how much leverage for change you can exert.
	Culture	Your working group may encourage innovation, or expect significant justification for any new initiative. Once approved, it may be impossible to secure approval for any changes that prove necessary.
Organisational	Institutional priorities	Linkage to institutional priorities will make it easier to secure the go-ahead and also to find collaborators. You might connect the development to your institution's learning and teaching strategy.
	Funding	Funding provides time and resources to deliver the project, and draw in colleagues. Such funding may also make it easier to link up with educational developers from within your institution, whose expertise you can tap into and learn from.
Sector	National priorities	Other resources may well have been developed in the area, and larger-scale funding may become available. For funding of projects within the UK, see under www.connect.ac.uk.

Might it have been a rather less enthralling experience than I have just suggested? Did you feel threatened at being confronted with new materials? Did they seem semi-digested, and not in line with the learning outcomes? Riddled with infelicities of style? Were they idiosyncratic, a departure from the 'normal' sequence and hard to follow? Was the approach, frankly, wacky? Did it savour of innovation for its own sake? Most of us can readily identify with such scenarios.

I can recall instances when the materials that a colleague produced for me to deliver reached me at a point that allowed insufficient preparation time – such as the occasions when they appeared under the door part-way through a two-hour class. That they appeared before the end of the class was, perhaps, a triumph on the part of my colleague, but this did not contribute to my equanimity. Not only that but the materials were so inordinately clever that I had difficulty understanding them, let alone being able to explain them to the students. We often learn through our teaching, but feeling mystified about a text or a technique is not a sound basis for gaining the confidence of one's students. I nonetheless survived, as did they.

Of course we all want our colleagues to report back that the class that hitherto has always had them in despair has been transformed into a roaring success, all due to our inspired materials. This might conceivably happen, or it might not. However, it is more likely to occur if we can avoid colleagues delivering our materials with hesitation and embarrassment.

The way to help colleagues take ownership of materials, other than producing the goods on time, is to consult them and involve them in the process. Not only is that likely to help them view your materials positively, it is likely to give people space to think them through. You may even find they provide you with feedback, coming up with ideas you can incorporate, or maybe their eagle eye can enable you to purge the materials of some of those otherwise embarrassing typos and non sequiturs. Your colleagues may well then trial the materials from a position of involvement.

This is the joyous side of teamwork; at this point, you, the proud creator, step back after hours of hard labour and hear your colleague explain to others the intricacies of the materials you slaved over for hours, and for which he or she contributed a few minor adjustments. Lips sealed, you listen to your colleague taking the credit. But isn't that what you wanted, to get your colleague involved?

Hilary Rollin, Department of Modern Languages,
Oxford Brookes University

EVALUATING AND DISSEMINATING THE DEVELOPMENT

It may be tempting to leave any consideration of the evaluation of your project until towards the end, but evaluation is too important to be left as an after-thought, and needs to be addressed right alongside the initial planning. This stems in part from the need to collect data at appropriate points: as the students embark on their learning and at appropriate staging points on the way. Evaluation is thus closely linked to monitoring progress on your project, which Baume (2003) defines as follows:

> At its heart, monitoring is a very simple and common process. It runs alongside, or indeed is integral to or frequently interspersed with, most conscious human activities. Monitoring involves first asking a question such as 'How is it going?'
>
> Given some answers to this question, monitoring further involves asking and answering a further question along the lines of: 'So (how) should we change what we are doing?'
>
> (p. 77)

More rigorous evaluation certainly requires you to adopt a well-thought-out methodology, perhaps along the lines of Saunders (2000). We have already seen in Chapter 4 that student feedback forms usually provide only limited information. Your existing views on what works are unlikely to be challenged very much in this situation. One will usually need to go beyond this level of evaluation, drawing on data from a variety of sources to improve the reliability of your findings through triangulation. Yet such evaluation is essential if the development is to serve your practice more widely, and indeed be of much use to colleagues.

In this case dissemination is also required, and again this needs to be built in right from the start. The most effective way to disseminate a development is to involve those you would like to find out about the project right from the very beginning, as we have already seen in the Case study 8.2. If colleagues actually contribute to what is planned, they will certainly find out about what is going on, and are more likely to be ready to trial or adapt your materials and ideas. Of course, this is not always possible, but for maximum impact of a development this mindset is essential.

You may, however, also want to disseminate knowledge about your development by writing for publication. This is, of course, particularly important if your work is to provide evidence for excellence in teaching, given the way in which publications often involve peer review or reach a national or international audience. Experts on writing (see, for instance, Boice, 1990) suggest that you should build regular opportunities to write in to your weekly schedule rather than simply relying on a binge approach, as a more regular approach is easier to sustain in the longer run and leads to higher levels of productivity. It will help in this if you can divide larger writing tasks into more manageable sub-tasks, and this in turn indicates a need to structure your writing fairly early on. You may also find it helpful to engage others in this process rather than viewing writing as a solitary activity, so that you respond to feedback and take account of your intended audience more directly. The audience is essential to such writing – if a paper is intended for an educational journal, for instance, your development will clearly need to have been evaluated in a robust fashion, an issue we shall consider later in this chapter.

PROJECT MANAGING THE DEVELOPMENT

This development cycle of design, implementation, evaluation and dissemination provides a basis for carrying out a project, but each of these phases can be assisted by more broad expertise in project management. Many developments in teaching comprise activity that can be said to be bounded in time, with specific associated goals and resources. It thus makes sense to view a development as a project. The need for project management is now widely accepted across both the private and public sectors. Many projects fail, and for a wide variety of reasons: over time or budget, implementation not approved, redundancy of deliverables, user needs not met or insufficient take-up, staff leaving the project team at a critical juncture, and so on. Techniques, however, have been developed to manage the risks involved, and it is to these that we now turn. The scale of the projects envisaged here will not usually require use of the sophisticated protocols that exist for planning complex projects, but we will still benefit from some basic principles of project management.

The first lesson is that project planning is critical: you need to set clear goals that you can identify have been met (see also Chapter 4). Some projects distinguish between general aims, more qualitative

TABLE 8.2 Specifying the nature and timing of the activity that comprises the project

Work-breakdown and scheduling	Comment
Specify the activity that needs to occur in order to deliver the goals of the project	This helps to ensure that work is not forgotten, that it occurs in an appropriate order, to an appropriate timetable – and if you are able to, that responsibilities can be allocated to those involved in the development.
Categorise the activity	This helps to ensure some coherence across the project.
Specify who will carry out which activity	Clarity is essential to ensure that everything is covered.
Resources that are needed to deliver the activities	You may find that some work cannot go ahead if further resources are not secured. This may affect which activity you carry out at which point.
Timing for each activity to be carried out, with indication of key deadlines	Key deadlines may include approval, printing, distribution of materials to students, as well as the actual start of teaching.

outcomes that are more difficult to measure, and deliverables – the materials, events, training, and so on that the project provides. Specifying what you hope to achieve through the project in this fashion, even at a modest level of detail, then enables you to identify the work that is entailed, as we see in Table 8.2. Of course, you can again specify the work involved at different levels of detail. But it remains important to break down the work involved, even if only to a modest degree.

It is also important to manage the associated risks, and the factors that will influence the success of the project. What would seriously damage the project? Do you have a reliable process in place that will enable you to achieve the goals? What will happen if you fail to secure the necessary approval for introducing the new module? What will happen if the students fail to engage during the early sessions? What could you do about this? Table 8.3 gives a few examples of different risks, as well as factors that are likely to influence the success of the

TABLE 8.3 Chart to analyse risk and success factors, with examples

Scale of impact	Chance of occurring	Strategy to reduce risk or maximise success
Key colleague on the project may pull out		
End of project delayed by at least four months	Several colleagues left last academic year	Ensure that work is collaborative so that someone else is able to take over
Approval not granted, or granted only under certain conditions		
End of project; or project is completed but without enthusiasm	Total rejection unlikely, but conditions could easily be set	Involve at least one committee member in the project, and sort out issues in advance with committee chair
Project sponsor changes their mind		
End of project; or significant work is wasted	Sponsor occasionally goes back on earlier decisions	Keep the sponsor informed about progress, and ask them to exercise influence on key issues
Students really enjoy the new course unit		
Further developments may follow on afterwards	Quite likely	Convey confidence and enthusiasm during the early stages; pay attention to professionalism

project. After all, if you can identify key things that will enhance the impact of your project, then you are likely to be able to target your effort more effectively. In particular, there may be a person who is sponsoring your project, and the extent to which they are happy with the progress of the project is perhaps more important than any other factor. You might try to complete a version of Table 8.3 for your own project.

Finally here, we highlight the fact that colleagues have a significant impact on the success or failure of a project itself, as well as on the extent to which the development is disseminated. A project sponsor may be key in this, but so may many other colleagues. You will need to give some thought as to how you might involve them in the project or reduce potential opposition, even if it is well intentioned. It is thus worth considering the following questions for your project:

- Who are the major stakeholders in your project?
  - What are their needs and interests?
  - How can you involve them in the project?
- Whose opposition should you try to avoid?
  - What might underlie their attitude to your project?
  - How can you deal with these?

There are a range of other project management techniques that you can adopt – as, for instance, detailed in Baume *et al.* (2002) – including networking, use of a project steering group, resource management and team working. These are particularly worth considering where a number of colleagues are also involved.

BEYOND DEVELOPMENT AND INTO RESEARCH

It is one thing to carry out a development project successfully; it is something else completely to ensure that this becomes the basis for research into learning and teaching, with your study leading to widely applicable findings, or to carry out research into learning and teaching more broadly. We focus here on three issues that must be addressed for practitioners to progress towards research into their practice: interest, methodology and, for some practitioners, the readiness to undergo a paradigm shift.

Review point 8.2
GOING FOR IT

Identify an issue related to a development you are currently carrying out (or have recently carried out). What might prompt/might have prompted you to put an investigation into this issue in hand?

You evidently need the motivation: research requires dedication and a willingness to explore the issues, as Case study 8.3, by Mònica Feixas, illustrates. If this is all in addition to your research within your discipline and, of course, to all the other duties that you have to carry out, then we can see why the transition from evaluation to more robust research is a challenging one to make.

Case study 8.3
ANSWERS TO QUESTIONS

I knew I had a good résumé, knowledge about teaching, some experience as a part-time associate teacher and a lot of enthusiasm. I thought I was prepared to start teaching at university, but I was not.

I began by teaching two theoretical subjects. Many of the students were older and more experienced than me. The course content had already been established and contextualised to the Catalan reality, so I could not easily change topics or apply what I had learnt during my postgraduate studies. In addition, the experience of lecturing to a group of 70 students was very stressful at first. I felt unqualified and insecure, despite having a degree in teaching and a Masters degree in Educational Administration. The only way I could control the anxiety was to write my notes down and go through them line by line. I also felt quite lonely in the department, because I was working part-time. I could not attend many meetings or integrate myself into the departmental culture; and at that time there were no induction or mentoring programmes for new teachers.

One year later I got a full-time job in the department. By then I felt much more at home in the department, and more thoroughly prepared for my teaching; but I was still not satisfied. I wanted to become an outstanding university teacher. How could I motivate and help my students to become independent learners? What was the most appropriate methodological and assessment strategy according to the content of my subjects? I wanted answers to these questions, answers that could only come through research.

I also had some questions about my own experience and wanted to know if it was a unique experience or if other new teachers had similar anxieties. What sort of changes do university teachers go through? Should the university promote training initiatives to help them? Which ones would be the most appropriate? What type of departmental culture and leadership fosters teaching quality awareness? These questions provided a starting point for my Doctoral research. I first did a short study on the problems of beginning teachers, and this led on to work on the process of professional development for university teachers. I am pleased that this research has helped me and has now helped to improve the support for beginning teachers and the training of university teachers at my institution.

Mònica Feixas, Departament Pedagogia Aplicada,
Universitat Autònoma de Barcelona

Many developments are indeed limited to the immediate context in which they are carried out. Without a more systematic understanding of why something has worked, it is difficult to transfer lessons to other contexts. The first teaching development that one of us carried out was intended as an action research project, but the underpinning methodology was weak, and the data that was collected proved insufficient: it never saw publication in a peer-reviewed journal. It failed as a research project, although not in development terms, as it led to the student guide mentioned in Chapter 3. The major higher education journals face this situation on a large scale, with papers often coming into the category of poorly evaluated curriculum developments, relying often on an informal analysis of data from student feedback questionnaires and assessment results. Ashwin and Trigwell (2004), for instance, identify investigations that are designed to produce knowledge of relevance to oneself and local knowledge of relevance to one's colleagues. Meanwhile, investigations that produce public knowledge require explicit consideration of issues around validity and reliability; and this requires closer attention to methodology.

Developing understanding of the methodology is evidently essential when moving from development work to research. Thorough investigation of the different approaches to research and the available methodology is essential: the reader is advised to consult a relevant text, such as Cohen *et al.* (2000), Silverman (2001) or Knight (2002). One might be tempted to collect some data first of all, perhaps related to assessment (or certainly not something that requires too much work!), and then try to make sense of it using some methodology or other. But methodology quite clearly needs to come at a much earlier stage of the process, not least to ensure that the data you actually collect is appropriate to your research question. Indeed, the data will need to be rich enough to explore the issues around *why* this educational practice is effective or inadequate: a central issue in the extent to which your work can be seen to apply to other situations.

However, there is more to this than simply adopting new research methods: a paradigm shift also needs to occur, as Neill Thew describes in Case study 8.4. Tutors with a background in the social sciences will have something of an advantage, in that their academic expertise is already located in the relevant methodology. Research into learning and teaching is only able to offer conclusions that are relatively limited in extent, given the unpredictability of human behaviour and the myriad of concerns that actually shape day-to-day practice. Academics from the natural sciences, certainly, will be used to drawing conclusions that are more definitive in nature, and they are likely to need to adjust to the differences. Similarly, they may need to adjust to the use of qualitative research methods, as these methods can help to capture the complexity of educational experience. Yet, if we are to provide more robust evidence for the value of our development work, and to extend our understanding of how students learn, then we need to take steps into research.

Case study 8.4
FIRST STEPS INTO RESEARCH

How did I adapt to a new research paradigm when I first began to engage in research into my teaching? I think that the honest answer has to be slowly, hesitantly, painfully and with many false starts. Like many of us moving into a new research area, I did not really know for quite some time what it was that I did not know.

My academic background is in English literature and psychoanalysis. Give me a text, and I am in comfortably familiar territory. However, I still vividly remember attending my first teaching and learning – as opposed to English Studies – conference. My two lasting impressions are a sense of panic that I was a total fraud being there at all – half expecting at any moment to be exposed and booted out – and that the tone of the conference was considerably more collegial and less combative than I was used to.

My route into researching my own teaching was perhaps unusual. As a literary critic, I was interested in identities – what they were; how they came into being; and how they were subject to sometimes vicious contestation and debate. I came to realise that some of the same processes relating to ethnicity and gender that I was analysing in texts were being played out before me in my classrooms, and that my own presence and behaviours were significantly involved in these dynamics. I found this insight personally hugely challenging, and could not leave it alone.

My first steps, then, were to see what research skills I could transfer from studying texts to investigating my classrooms, pedagogy and practices.

I am not sure quite how consciously planned this was: I was just, I think, reacting to wanting to explore an idea in the way that seemed natural to me. My research perspective was essentially invisible to me. I certainly was not explicitly asking myself any epistemological questions about the nature of the research, evidence or 'truth' I was exploring.

As time went on and I began to encounter the scholarly field, I was able to locate my work and research assumptions within a wider context. Given that we all come to researching our own teaching from any number of different directions, then the things that challenge or surprise us are likely to differ considerably. Every year, the Postgraduate Certificate in Higher Education participants with whom I now work are challenged in a huge variety of ways as they come to find themselves in a territory between their own discipline and investigating their teaching. My own three challenges were: encountering quantitative work for the first time and not having a clue what these tests and columns of numbers really meant; being frustrated by what I read as an alarmingly prevalent apologetic tone in much teaching research; and having to grapple with the issue of finding myself an object of my own enquiry to a significantly greater degree than ever before (though, of course, working on identity had already required me to think carefully and systematically about my own).

Neill Thew, Teaching and Learning Development Unit, University of Sussex

CONCLUSION

Development projects and research into learning and teaching offer a real opportunity for you to take your teaching forward, allowing you to take responsibility for what happens, investigate what others have done before you, ponder what will work in your own context, seek to engage colleagues and convince them that they should join you, find out what students actually think, analyse your practice more rigorously and share your experience with others. The public dimension to a project or to research may also enable you to establish a reputation for excellent teaching, opening up further opportunities to develop your teaching, as we shall see in Chapter 9.

Meanwhile, in this present chapter, we have seen how projects and research can provide a genuine route into a scholarly approach to teaching. Trigwell and Shale (2004) describe a scholarship of teaching with three temporal components: *awareness* of conceptions of practice, knowledge itself and development processes; the *ability* to carry out developments that involve investigation, reflection, collaboration and learning; and a readiness to deliver *outcomes* that move teaching in the discipline forward, provide the developer with satisfaction, leave artefacts behind and so on (see also Ashwin and Trigwell, 2004). Investigation is a central element in achieving scholarship of this depth, offering a rich vein of interactions with knowledge, practice, students and colleagues. We see how a scholarly approach to teaching can stand alongside our subject research as an activity in which we can invest ourselves.

REFERENCES

Ashwin, P. and Trigwell, K. (2004) 'Investigating Staff and Educational Development', in Baume, D. and Kahn, P. E. (eds) *Enhancing Staff and Educational Development*. London: RoutledgeFalmer, 117–31.

Baume, D. (2003) 'Monitoring and Evaluating Staff and Educational Development', in Kahn, P. E. and Baume, D. (eds) *A Guide to Staff and Educational Development*. London: Kogan Page, 76–95.

Baume, C., Martin, P. and Yorke, M. (2002) *Managing Educational Development Projects*. London: Kogan Page.

Boice, R. (1990) *Professors as Writers: A Self-help Guide to Productive Writing*. Stillwater, OK: New Forums.

Cohen, L., Manion, L. and Morrison, K. (2000) *Research Methods in Education*, fifth edition. London: RoutledgeFalmer.

Gustavsen, B. (2001) 'Theory and Practice: The Mediating Discourse', in Reason, P. and Bradbury, H. *Handbook of Action Research*. London: Sage, 17–26.

Kahn, P. E. and Baume, D. (eds) (2003) *A Guide to Staff and Educational Development*. London: Kogan Page.

Knight, P. (2002) *Small-scale Research*. London: Sage.

Roche, V. (2003) 'Being an Agent of Change', in Kahn, P. E. and Baume, D. (eds) *A Guide to Staff and Educational Development*. London: Kogan Page, 171–91.

Saunders, M. (2000) 'Beginning an Evaluation with RUFDATA: Theorising an Approach to Evaluation Planning'. *Evaluation*, 6, 1, 7–21.

Silverman, D. (2001) *Interpreting Qualitative Data: Methods for Analysing Talk, Text and Interaction*, second edition. London: Sage.

Trigwell, K. and Shale, S. (2004) 'Student Learning and the Scholarship of University Teaching'. *Studies in Higher Education*, 29, 4, 523–36.

Chapter 9

Teaching development roles

> Leadership and learning are inseparable in universities. Genuine learning requires an atmosphere of trust and an absence of fear; in these circumstances academics, like their students, take risks, improve, and do remarkable things.
>
> (Ramsden, 1998: 268)

INTRODUCTION

The collaborative nature of higher education means that many developments in teaching are taken forward by a group of colleagues. Taking on a role that allows you to lead the development of teaching within your institution can thus significantly increase your scope to initiate change. Your ideas will be taken more seriously, and you will have greater scope to shape the way in which they are implemented. Certainly, younger staff may find it difficult to convince colleagues to take new ideas on board, or that an initial idea bears little resemblance to what actually happens.

Capacity for development more broadly is related to your ability to create links with other people, as Gustavsen (2001) argues. He points out that new ideas are often stimulated by discussions or work with others, as are strategies to overcome challenges in development work. The richer and denser your relationships with others in the field, the greater will be the fund of ideas on which to draw. A development role can provide access to new networks, extending your range of potential collaborators, and we have already seen in Chapter 6 the value of such networks.

In theory, taking on a development role can also free up time, a precious commodity in the pressured world of higher education. Even if in practice one's teaching or administrative load is not fully adjusted to reflect the demands of the role, or not adjusted at all, a clear responsibility does at least provide a reason to channel energy in the direction of developing your teaching.

We will thus look in this chapter at ways in which you can use a specific responsibility for teaching as a focus for development, once you have initially gained it. Indeed, gaining an appropriate role may take real effort, particularly if a promotion is required to reach a sufficient level of seniority. We devote particular attention to how you should go about claiming excellence in your teaching. The manner in which you carry out the role is also important, as is a sense of direction to your career – otherwise frustration is likely to mount. You will simply find that other doors – where you could have focused more fruitful effort – have been closed to you. First of all, however, it will help to possess a keen appreciation for the different roles that are available; and it is to these that we now turn.

WHAT ARE THE OPTIONS?

The list of teaching responsibilities is a long and familiar one. Responsibilities can come at module, programme, departmental, school, faculty or university level: Programme Leader, membership of a teaching committee, Teaching Fellowship, Disability Officer, Senior Tutor, Examinations Officer, Director of Undergraduate Studies, Learning Technology Adviser and so on. The titles for different roles will, of course, vary from university to university – but the substance is often the same. Assessment, quality assurance, pastoral care of students and organisation of teaching provide the basis for a range of roles, whether involving undergraduates or postgraduates. Even in the most junior of settings, there is likely to be some post open to the interested member of staff, even acting as a representative for the graduate teaching assistants in a department, for example. And at the other end of the spectrum, there are National Teaching Fellowships, in England at least, and even Professorships granted largely on the basis of excellence in teaching.

Such roles offer varying scope for the development of teaching and lead to different outcomes. It therefore makes sense to consider some of the benefits of these roles, perhaps to assist in choosing which roles to target and which to avoid; this will also influence how you subsequently carry out the role:

- Politics – some roles involve limited opportunities for development because of the immediate politics. A more senior colleague may be ready to block new initiatives or the immediate post-holder may still wield a good deal of influence.
- Authority – different posts also carry with them varying levels of authority or influence. You may simply have less scope to initiate change in certain areas without incurring opposition.
- Relationships – a role will open up access to a specific group of staff, so you need to be aware of who you are likely to have to work with, whether colleagues who have little interest in teaching or those who are keen to share ideas on how to develop their teaching.
- Institutional knowledge – relationships with others can also facilitate involvement in the life of the institution, which, as Boice (1992) notes, is critical to longer-term success. You may have scope to get to know key people, to find out what it takes to secure scarce resources or to build alliances An examinations role, for instance, might not facilitate this in the way that a quality enhancement role could.
- Profile – some roles offer greater scope to make a name for yourself: establishing a new Masters degree programme may count for more than keeping happy the students who are already there.

SECURING A DEVELOPMENT ROLE

Given this range of factors, which are all in some way situated within a wider social or cultural context, it will be important to take a proactive approach to which teaching responsibilities you take on. It might easily be the case that a role is simply foisted on to you, so it makes sense to position yourself to avoid roles you would rather not take on and to land a role that you would like. A mentor can be particularly useful in this, helping you to decide the direction in which you would like to move, as we considered in Chapter 7.

You may have a clear appreciation of the direction you would like to take, but colleagues may have quite different perceptions. Appointments are often made on this more implicit social basis – if colleagues are aware of your relevant experience, then you may be seen as the heir apparent. Colleagues may need to be convinced of your suitability in terms of expertise and prior experience, perhaps with a mentor acting as an advocate for you. On one level it may help simply to express an interest, in either the role itself or even the general area in which the role is situated, but a more sophisticated approach may be needed.

A model that is helpful in analysing awareness within the process of human interaction is the Johari Window, as outlined in Figure 9.1. This window describes four different aspects of awareness: the open area, which represents things that I know about myself and that others know about me; the blind area, representing things that others know about me but of which I myself am blind to; the hidden area, for things that I know about myself but do not reveal to others; and finally the unknown area, containing things of which neither I nor others are aware. It is easy to assume that the open area is larger than it actually is, as much of what we imagine is known to others is in fact hidden from them. The challenge then is to develop the trust needed to be more open with our colleagues and, when appropriate, with our students, as we saw earlier in Chapter 3, about our motivations, experiences, attitudes, values and so on. You will also need to welcome feedback from colleagues in this area, reducing the size of the blind area in order to

	Known to self	Not known to self
Known to others	**Open area**	**Blind area**
Not known to others	**Hidden area**	**Unknown area**

FIGURE 9.1 The Johari Window

Source: After Luft, 1970.

increase the size of the open area. This provides a much more realistic basis to display expertise or interest in a given aspect of teaching.

A further option is to create your own role, perhaps on the basis of an innovative approach to student learning. This is an approach that Linda Altshul took, as she describes in Case study 9.1. Taking the initiative in this way allows you greater control over your future development path, and being able to demonstrate that you are actively involved in a number of roles can also help in avoiding being 'volunteered' for potentially less desirable positions! If colleagues can see that you have the capacity to introduce new initiatives, then it is quite possible that you will be given further rein to carry out development work, perhaps without the administrative load that is attached to more established responsibilities.

Case study 9.1
HOW THE TEAM OF TEACHERS RAN

We had three parallel classes running; and how the team of teachers ran! At the end of each tutored self-access class on the English as a Foreign Language programme we were left exhilarated by the buzz from the interaction. We started each class separately with a short activity to widen learner awareness of possible approaches to studying a particular language skill. Then students chose a task and could study in any of four equipped self-access rooms, with the tutors advising and answering questions. Each session ended with a whole-group review of what had been learned.

This approach had emerged from my interest in the growing international research and practice in self-access language learning that I had learned about during my own postgraduate studies. After collecting and disseminating evidence of the benefits, I was asked to co-ordinate a working group to develop the programme. I introduced the team-teaching described above to enable on-going training for teachers who were new to the ideas. We had staff development workshops and regular meetings, both face to face and via email. Other teachers contributed to the development of the programme ideas as their own enthusiasm and experience grew. The programme became known as Developing Independent Language Learning (DILL).

The growing success of DILL and the opening of the multimedia Language Resource Centre led to a request by the Head of School that I should make a proposal to widen and adapt the application to the whole school through personal tutoring. His authority backed up my recommendations, which were accepted. I was asked to chair the school-wide working group that rolled out DILL to all language students. Concurrently I made a successful bid for external funding to look into the effects of DILL on student progression and retention. This bought time so that I could increase staff development activities across the school and also enabled making DILL materials available on a VLE.

The effects of the DILL approach are radical not only with the learners but also with staff. While there remains a minority who have yet to be convinced, DILL has introduced many colleagues to a learner-centred approach. A typical tutor said, 'I felt a bit out of my depth' during the first year. However, confidence and skills have grown through both experience and an extensive staff development programme, which colleagues now help to lead. Another tutor's comment exemplifies the impact of the DILL programme: 'The interest is in seeing how students think. The closer we can get to their view of how they are learning, the better we can teach – or rather get them to learn.'

My role in advancing staff development and use of e-learning led to a secondment as Faculty Learning Technologies Fellow. I now continue to promote a learner-centred focus in the use of the VLE in other disciplines in the training sessions that I run across the faculty.

Linda Altshul, School of Languages, Salford University

You might also consider whether it is worth establishing a network of colleagues in your institution or department who want to develop their teaching, drawing on the advice given in Chapter 6 on networking. Take a lead role, set up a committee, organise workshops or seminars, get colleagues involved. Set up a virtual meeting point for colleagues interested in researching their teaching practice, or set up and lead a research group. Got the idea? So take a look around and consider the kinds of action you might take.

Review point 9.1
ASSESSING YOUR KNOWLEDGE

1 Choose three different aspects of your teaching where you have particular interest, ability or experience, and assess the scope that each aspect offers for taking on further responsibility.

2 Complete a Johari window for the most promising of these three aspects, by assessing how much knowledge is present in each area of the window (except of course for the 'Unknown area'!), and by providing examples of knowledge contained within each area. For the 'Blind area' you will clearly need help from one or more colleagues. If you subsequently revisit this exercise you should be able to reduce the size of the unknown area.

3 How can you increase the trust with your colleagues that fosters disclosure of your hidden knowledge? How can you gain feedback on your work in this area from your colleagues?

Some roles, however, are specifically awarded on the basis of a specific claim to excellence, often brought together through a teaching portfolio. Promotions to senior or principal lecturer typically require claims to excellence, and, where the claim is based in significant part on teaching, are likely to lead to further responsibility for teaching; this is certainly common in the hierarchical setting of higher education. Convincing claims do not simply appear out of the ether; they need to be created and shaped. So we focus here on several issues that need to be addressed in staking a convincing claim.

1 *Collect an appropriate set of information*. The first challenge is to gather together a set of information that relates to the criteria that will be used to assess your claim. (Processes to judge excellence in teaching that do not employ explicit criteria should now be a thing of the past.) Your claims will be more convincing if you can point to the independent nature of the evidence, and to the way in which different perspectives or types of data all point to the same conclusion. Table 9.1 lists examples of sources on which you might wish to draw. It will help if you keep a record of your continuing professional development each year, perhaps supported by a folder where you collect together evidence that relates to your teaching.

2 *Ground specific claims within the data*. As a starting point it makes sense to take a look at the data you have collected on your teaching, to see what claims might most obviously arise from the information. Certainly, abstract claims that are not directly linked to the information about your teaching will hardly be taken seriously. You need to

TABLE 9.1 Sources of data on your teaching

Examples	Comment
Aspects of teaching	
Classroom teaching, course design, creating the learning environment, assessment	A focus on the developments you have led in relevant areas will be essential
Statistical data	
Assessment results, teaching load, scores from student evaluation questionnaires	A claim may be more convincing if the data is considered relative to colleagues (e.g. twice the average departmental load for teaching)
Stakeholder views	
Peer observation, data from student evaluation questionnaires, quality assurance reports, employer views	Views provided by others are generally looked on favourably
Research into teaching	
Publications, presentations, funding, grants, projects	Research on the effectiveness of your own teaching can be particularly compelling
Responsibilities	
Module Leader, Programme Leader, departmental roles, specific initiative that you have led	Information about how you developed teaching is again essential
Recognition	
Qualifications in teaching, involvement in professional bodies, awards	Recognition can come at different levels, from departmental to institutional and beyond

point out the specific ways in which the data backs up your claims, citing or referring to examples, patterns and so on from within the data. Information about your teaching only becomes evidence for excellence when directly linked to specific claims about your teaching. You cannot assume that someone else will see the links that you see.

3 *Link your claims directly to the criteria*. It is important to make sure that the claims relate quite closely to the criteria. Some claims will be more relevant than others, even while still being true and important in

the abstract – just not important in this context. For instance, the criteria might look for evidence of leadership; and you will thus need to take care in the way in which you present collaborative work. Therefore, it is also important to analyse every single claim you make in light of the criteria. You will also want to look through the data to seek to generate claims with each criteria in mind.

4 *Draw on theoretical perspectives in shaping the claims*. Educational research involves more than looking for patterns within a set of data. Not only is this too open a process to avoid personal bias creeping in, it may lead to missing important perspectives. Indeed, if you want to take things a stage further, you may find it helpful to draw on research methods from the social sciences (see, for instance, Cohen *et al.*, 2000).

You can also shape claims in the light of one or more theoretical perspectives. This could certainly give your case a distinctive edge on the competition. Have you based any of your teaching on a given theoretical perspective – perhaps on experiential learning? You would be able to make an exceptionally strong case if you could demonstrate that across the board your teaching stems from an advanced conception teaching, linked as this is to clear research evidence for effective teaching. One of the advantages of drawing on a theoretical perspective is that you can call on evidence from research to support your claim to excellence. If this is borne out in independent evidence from assessment, students or colleagues, then the case will be exceptional.

5 *Ensure coherence across a set of claims*. In making a claim for excellence in teaching, you are essentially constructing an argument. It will be important that your argument is based on a coherent shape, perhaps derived from some overarching perspectives. You can, of course, simply look for patterns within your individual claims, but you may find it helps to draw more directly on one or more principles that organise your claims within an overall statement. With greater coherence, you are then in a position to pick and choose between different claims, so that you can highlight the key claims and discard peripheral claims.

6 *Take account of your audience*. You will, finally, need to take account of the audience for your claim; this will help you to choose what to emphasise, taking more immediate account of the actual group of people who will judge your claim. Who are they? What are their interests?

TABLE 9.2 Strategies to achieve coherence across a set of claims

Coherence stems from	Comment
Your personal philosophy of teaching	Roots your claim in your identity as a teacher. It is here that we begin to address a more substantive basis for excellent teaching, for instance, going beyond an ability to manipulate student feedback.
The criteria themselves	The claims are directly structured to follow the criteria – you address each criteria in turn.
Characteristics of the data set	The data itself might suggest a structure – perhaps stakeholder perspectives, different levels of recognition for your teaching or so on.
Theory	One or more theoretical perspectives may enable you to develop coherence across a number of claims.
Institutional priorities	Claims can be structured around institutional concerns or priorities, which are likely to appeal to those who will make the judgements, such as improving the efficiency of teaching, respecting student diversity or attracting international students.
'Spin'	It is easy to inflate your own achievements! You should be able fully to substantiate every claim that you make; adding qualifications where required.

In this regard it will help for a colleague to review your claim, perhaps to make challenges but also to identify your strengths. As Case study 9.2 indicates, this is often the key issue in making a claim for excellence.

7 *Revise the claim.* Published work normally goes through a whole range of revisions. If your claim is genuinely to reach a professional standard, you will need to polish and revise the text again and again, and again. You may well want to ask a colleague or mentor to help in this process, something that Simon Lightfoot found helpful in Case study 9.2.

Review point 9.2
VIEWPOINTS

Identify three different principles you could apply to provide coherence across a claim for excellence in your teaching as a whole. Identify which principle might be best to apply when the claim is to be read by an audience of: (a) Vice-chancellors; (b) parents of your students; and (c) research-oriented colleagues.

Case study 9.2
CLAIMING SUCCESS AT TEACHING

I sent an initial draft of my application for an institutional Teaching Fellowship to a colleague for comments. She highlighted that I needed to demonstrate and provide evidence of excellence in teaching, but my draft did neither!

The hardest thing was to overcome a classic British reserve – making claims for individual excellence is not something I do every day. Even writing this case study still feels odd. So much of my day-to-day work involves team work; and I felt that making an individual claim meant underestimating the considerable efforts of my colleagues. As a result my initial draft read more like an application by the politics team than by an individual.

So with my colleague's comments ringing in my head, I collected together plenty of information on my teaching, and tried to see how it all related to the criteria for excellence. At first I found it easier to find evidence for dissemination – there were concrete events and publications to which I could point. I also found evidence that I could apply theory to my teaching; I had already consciously drawn on theory to help shape my work, so doing this was relatively easy.

However, I found it more difficult to tackle the general issue of how I had helped students to learn. I imagine that part of the problem lies with the time pressures of working in higher education. While I acknowledge the benefits of reflective practice, it is often only linked to identifying solutions to 'problems' – Why did that assessment not seem to work? Why did the students react in that way? – rather than reflecting on success.

I began, though, to look for issues related to student learning within the evidence from peer review, institutional student surveys, informal student feedback, post-it-notes and so on across a number of modules and levels; and I soon came across the evidence I needed. Informal student comments about induction procedures that I had suggested, formal student feedback on the benefits of formative assessments that I had introduced, and a peer review on the learner-focused approach in my classes; all these showed that I had the ability to help students learn.

Claiming success is not something that comes naturally to many people and I am no different. However, the process of sitting down and reflecting on your teaching practice and realising that you do make a difference is extremely rewarding. You also realise that it provides for further developments in your own practice.

Finally, it is worth noting that in putting a claim together you may see that there are certain gaps in your experience or expertise. You can thus gain insight into your own strengths and weaknesses, enabling you to plan your development or to look for further relevant experience. The process itself of making the claim can thus lead you to develop your teaching, even if you do not actually go ahead with the application or receive the award.

Simon Lightfoot, School of Social Science, Liverpool John Moores University

TAKING ON A NEW ROLE

At some point you are likely to take on a specific role that actually allows you scope to develop teaching, even if the role is not one that you initially wanted; alternatively, you may have begun to carve out a role of your own making. The early period of your appointment generally sets the tone for ongoing work. If you are simply learning to manage one crisis after the next, then you will be unlikely to introduce many new developments. Or if you find that you hardly have any time to do more than keep the role ticking over, then again this will set the scene for your later work. Induction into the role is thus critical. Even if you do not have a formal mentor, you have a natural excuse to talk to others in similar roles, either in your own institution or beyond, about the opportunities and pitfalls of the role. For instance, an idea on how to protect or save your time could pay real dividends.

A responsibility for teaching can, however, easily become a maintenance function rather than an occasion for leadership. The difference resides in the way that you carry out a role rather than the role itself. Even what you might think of as mundane roles can allow scope for development opportunities. A number of positions come up regularly within departments, including those of quality assurance officer and disability support officer, but do not accept these roles just for the sake of doing something. Pay lip service to a responsibility and it may become a tiresome chore. Actively engage with it as a positive learning opportunity and it will become a valuable aspect of your practice.

It will therefore be worth looking more broadly at advice on exercising leadership in higher education, enabling you to motivate colleagues and make things happen. Ramsden (1998) argues that it is essential to be clear about what you want to achieve. Vision and good ideas are essential, enabling you to convince others to invest their energy in the direction that you have set. Without this vision, ongoing problems can only too easily sap your energy. This vision can be complemented by a belief in your own ability to make things happen, whatever the obstacles – a factor that is critical to developing teaching more widely as we have already seen in Chapters 3 and 8.

Ramsden points out that the environment in which teaching is carried out is also critical – your colleagues need to feel that they are trusted, that their contributions are valued and that their aspirations can be met, so you also need to understand your colleagues' perceptions of a situation. As he notes (1998: 83): 'The credibility of the vision stems from the fact that it is in harmony with the aspirations of academic staff, which in turn arises from them being academics themselves.' You might pick out a tool from Chapter 4, or another chapter, and use it to review and evaluate the way in which you lead colleagues through your teaching development role, helping to ensure insight into your colleagues' attitudes and aspirations. It may also help to engage in a strategic planning process, modelled on Ramsden (1998: 235), as shown in Box 9.1.

Both Ramsden (1998) and Knight and Trowler (2001) point out that it is essential to learn to lead. Awareness of your own approach to leadership is not something that can be developed overnight. It will similarly take time to learn how to draw out your colleagues, so that they are willing to volunteer their perspectives and views. And beyond this, you will also need knowledge of educational practice, approaches to leadership, and your own context, as well as the experience needed to pull all of this together – as Turner and Bolman's research (1998, cited in Knight and Trowler, 2001: 167) proposes.

You need to create space in which to develop this vision and enable this learning. So even at the outset, you may have scope to negotiate what tasks you will actually take on as part of your role. It may be

Box 9.1
STRATEGIC PLANNING

Situation analysis

- What are the institutional or national trends that underpin change related to your role?
- Spell out the characteristics of the environment in which your role is situated. What interests and motivates your colleagues?
- How do you prefer to exercise leadership? Characterise several situations in which your leadership has been welcomed.

Outcome analysis

- What student learning needs are in most urgent need of attention?
- What do you want to achieve in this role? For yourself, for specific colleagues and for your team as a whole?
- What would colleagues and managers want you to achieve in this role?

Leadership agenda

- What is the gap between your current situation and the desired outcome?
- Set out your leadership agenda in light of the gap between these, detailing your priorities, strategies, dangers to avoid, and development needs.

possible to pass on some of the more routine functions to a more junior colleague. Early on, you might also introduce initiatives that mean you need to spend less time maintaining systems. Time spent on processes rather than content can be particularly beneficial, as even introducing a simple pro forma or standard letter can streamline a process, or allow it to be passed on to someone else. You may then need only to review the process rather than carry it out each time.

This brings us to time management – creating space to allow you to shape the role in light of your priorities, rather than simply reacting passively to the day-to-day demands of your role. You may find it helpful to adopt a range of time management exercises, developing your ability to manage your workload. Perhaps the first most important aspect of time management is actually to be aware of how you spend your time, as Julie Wray found in Case study 9.3: does it reflect your priorities? You will also find that if you continually move from one task to another, perhaps by accessing emails, taking phone calls or browsing the internet too frequently, then you will benefit from planning what you carry out when, and then protecting your plans. This can allow you to plan in key activities that otherwise might never happen, such as reading articles or other material that is related to the development side of your role, and to deliver on your priorities. The project management techniques that we discussed in Chapter 8 will also be worth adopting more widely in your work. Most staff in higher education fulfil a number of roles, making it important to manage your workload as a whole, an issue that the final case study explores.

Review point 9.3
TIME MANAGEMENT

Complete a log of how you spend your time for a week, indicating each task that you complete, when it starts and finishes, whether you planned to carry it out, and any particular notes (see the log made available within Chapman, 2002).

Case study 9.3
BALANCING MY WORKLOAD

When I first came into higher education four years ago I was confident that I would be able to balance my teaching with everything else entailed in a lecturing role. My development would just happen, as I was both crafted at reflexivity and experienced in research. Having come direct from health care practice I felt capable of meeting the challenges, organising my workload and being assertive about saying no.

Well, maybe it was no surprise that this did not happen. Within a year the demands of the job had overwhelmed me, and I was bogged down in what seemed like boring, cluttered and uncreative work. I was constantly problem-solving for students, and burdened by paperwork and the need to comply with university rules (and there are plenty). There seemed to be little time left even to plan my teaching, let alone read the relevant literature or develop anything. I was leading a Masters programme, and yet had no space to organise and develop the programme. My output of publications was considerably depleted in comparison to when I was in practice; and this certainly felt rather odd. I began to wonder how this had all happened.

It occurred to me after looking at my yearly workload-balance form that most of my time was spent on jobs that were allocated the lowest weighting. This was largely down to an aspect of my practice that I was not really equipped to deal with: my role as a PBL facilitator. This form of teaching was new to me, and while I had attended some training sessions and read the literature, actual practice of PBL with students proved overpowering. I had become consumed by the students' inability to work as a team and create a cohesive group dynamic, and had begun to adopt an approach to pastoral care that was far too matriarchal and 'hands on'.

I began to think about what strategies could be employed to enable the students to engage more appropriately in PBL and at the same time release me from a 'dependency role'. In talking to some students it struck me that they needed to take ownership, and through this realisation I was able to pull back and hand over PBL to the students. I began, for instance, to timetable my availability and I requested from students a clear purpose for any meetings. I had seen my role as a teacher to teach and lost sight of the process of learning and discovery. As well as improving my teaching, this has created more time to dedicate to the Masters programme and to my research.

Julie Wray, School of Nursing, Salford University

CONCLUSION

Teaching certainly offers immense scope for exercising leadership in proposing and implementing new ideas, drawing colleagues into the process and seeing the difference that your work can make for students. You clearly need to take responsibility for this process, deciding where and how to invest your effort, and where to hold back, perhaps staking your claim to an area through clearly recognised dynamism.

Moreover, the range of possible directions in which you can develop your teaching remains vast. Which ideas should you prioritise? Should you focus on assessment, the accessibility of your internet resources, the extent to which you foster a dialogue with your students? Or perhaps it is more important to introduce some recent research into a stale course unit. And there is immense choice in the way in which you can take development work forward within a given area. Who should you work with? How should you go about staking a more obvious claim to specific areas of expertise? Should you look for more authority or for additional resources? We undoubtedly need a sense of direction to our work if we are to reconcile all of the conflicting demands and the varied opportunities and if we are to channel our energy rather than allow it to dissipate. It is to these, and related, questions that we now turn in our concluding chapter.

REFERENCES

Boice, R. (1992) *The New Faculty Member*. San Francisco, CA: Jossey-Bass.

Chapman, A. (2002) *Time-log*, Online, accessed 10 August 2005, www.businessballs.com/timemanagement.htm

Cohen, L., Manion, L. and Morrison, K. (2000) *Research Methods in Education*, fifth edition. London: RoutledgeFalmer.

Gustavsen, B. (2001) 'Theory and Practice: The Mediating Discourse', in Reason, P. and Bradbury, H. (eds) *Handbook of Action Research*. London: Sage, 17–26.

Knight, P. and Trowler, P. (2001) *Departmental Leadership in Higher Education*. Buckingham: Society for Research into Higher Education/Open University Press.

Luft, J. (1970) *Group Processes: An Introduction to Group Dynamics,* second edition. Palo Alto, CA: National Press Books.

Ramsden, P. (1998) *Learning to Lead in Higher Education*. London: Routledge.

Seldin, P. (2004) *The Teaching Portfolio: A Practical Guide to Improved Performance and Promotion/Tenure Decisions*. Bolton, MA: Anker.

Turner, C. and Bolman, R. (1998) 'Analysing the Role of the Subject Head of Department in Secondary Schools in England and Wales'. *School Leadership and Management* 18, 3, 373–88.

Chapter 10

A sense of direction

> I go amongst the buildings of a city and I see a man hurrying along to what? The Creature has a purpose and his eyes are bright with it.
>
> (John Keats)

INTRODUCTION

Imagine arriving unexpectedly at a large intersection, with a whole series of different turnings that you could take. Some of the options would lead you straight into oncoming traffic although you might not instantly be able to tell which ones these are, others would be safe to take but lead you in the wrong direction, while one or two would actually get you to your destination. A clear sense of where you are headed, and a readiness to look at the road signs, would certainly help you in choosing the right route.

We have seen an array of ways to develop your teaching in this book. There are processes that rely on you taking the initiative, and those that are triggered by your professional responsibilities. Some processes involve colleagues, while others are more solitary. We have considered reflective approaches, and actions that you can carry out. The scale can range from significant ongoing responsibility for teaching to short exercises that you can carry out in five minutes. We have offered plenty of ideas for developing your teaching – but should you adopt this method from Chapter 5 or that strategy from Chapter 8? Should you embark on a project that will soak up all your 'spare' time, or review your existing practice instead? We need to ensure that we do more than randomly respond to circumstances.

This concluding chapter looks at the effectiveness of the choices that we make. After all, we need to be able to actually get somewhere. This means that we need to learn which development processes actually work for us, and in which circumstances. However, such insight on its own will hardly give us a sense of direction: we also need a clear vision of where we are headed in developing our teaching, and a readiness to live out this vision.

LEARNING WHAT WORKS FOR YOU

We are aware that our students need to understand how they learn if they are to manage their learning effectively and to succeed in higher education; a similar principle also holds for learning about our own teaching. Can you see any pattern emerging in the way you have responded to this book, and to the review points within it? Perhaps you expected us as authors to do all of the running, avoiding any activity on your own part. If you did try out a number of the reviews, perhaps you can notice whether the ones you avoided had anything in common, or which ones benefited you the most – perhaps those involving interaction with colleagues. Megginson (1994) noted two patterns of learning that are particularly evident in the context of professional development: planned and emergent learning. He proposes that some people plan their learning quite deliberately, establishing at the outset the direction that their future learning will take and setting goals (see, for instance, development processes on pages 25, 55, 103, 125). In contrast to such planned learning, others are ready to take advantage of the opportunities to learn as they arise (evident on pages 16, 40, 53, among others), as we noted earlier in Chapter 1.

Megginson, particularly, encourages learners to take on forms of learning to which they are not naturally inclined. You might thus try a specific exercise from within this book, perhaps one to which you are not naturally inclined, and use this as a basis for learning about the way in which you develop your teaching – perhaps the exercise on assumption hunting or the questionnaires on learning styles, all referred to within Chapter 4.

As well as fitting our own learning style, specific development processes will be particularly well suited to your own personal context. You will thus need to take into account this context when choosing which development process to employ. Table 10.1 introduces some of the issues.

Review point 10.1
REVISITING

Revisit a proposed activity that you avoided when reading this book, and carry it out. What did you learn from actually doing this? Did the activity prove easier than you had imagined, or more difficult? Can you account for how it unfolded?

DEVELOPING YOUR TEACHING: AN ONGOING STORY

We will, though, still find that several different development processes are likely to work in any given set of circumstances. Of course, we are all used to choosing from among a number of possible options – but what else guides us in these choices other than their immediate effectiveness? Are we left with an entirely subjective approach that depends in large part on day-to-day whims and that changes as our circumstances shift, perhaps with every new departmental policy or Vice-Chancellor?

In addressing these issues, it is worth remembering that you are the one who has to make the choices and live with the consequences. This means that there needs to be a match between your choices and what you genuinely value. We cannot simply look for a technical solution: a categorisation as a certain type of learner or an assessment of likely effectiveness. Palmer (1998: 10) argues that understanding your own identity as a teacher is essential if you want to thrive, but this self-awareness is not something that is automatically ours. We need to explore what drives us – both in our academic and in the rest of our lives – if we are to understand which developments might turn out to be dead ends or lead us in the wrong direction altogether, resulting only in frustration.

Our aspirations for the future comprise a significant part of our identity as teachers and academics, helping us to determine where we are headed in developing our teaching. In many ways our aim is simply to teach well, and thus to help students learn effectively. In this book our primary focus has been on the process of developing your teaching. We could have tried to present an ideal vision of how to support student learning and then identified how to reach it, but instead we chose to

TABLE 10.1 Analysis of contextual factors that will affect our choice of which development process to employ

Contextual factor	Comments
Institution	Institutional policies, procedures, strategies, resources, and even the personalities of those in positions of authority are particularly relevant where larger-scale developments are concerned. For instance, the prospect of some project funding may tip you over into introducing a new development.
Department or school	Your immediate working culture has a significant influence on which developments are possible. You might well be reluctant to put a good deal of work into an innovative approach if you are convinced the relevant committee will never approve it.
Support from colleagues	The extent to which colleagues are interested in teaching will affect how social your approach can be and its scale (e.g. learning from others or working with others versus self-evaluation).
Requirement to engage	Some processes present themselves to us as a regular part of our work (e.g. peer review or mentoring). It may thus often make sense to choose to engage with these more fully, rather than taking on another process as well, only superficially.
Aspect of teaching	Some processes will be more suited than others to developing given aspects of our practice. For example, areas that involve relationships with others (e.g. personal tutoring, working with students who have disabilities) may particularly benefit from more social processes.
Depth of insight	Some situations are complex and require significant insight for development to occur. Processes involving more sustained levels of reflection thus provide a more adequate basis to transform such practice (e.g. appreciative enquiry or dealing with an issue through a critical collaboration).

focus on *how* to develop your teaching; on the process rather than the end point. Nonetheless, our discussion has identified certain aspects of good teaching. It will be worth picking out some of the threads that have been evident within different chapters as to what good teaching might look like:

- *Good teaching maintains a focus on student learning.* After all, it is the students who learn, and no teacher can force this. The research on conceptions of teaching that we noted in Chapter 3 provides robust evidence for the value of centring your teaching on the student, something also evident across all of the chapters. Case study 2.1, for instance, on fieldwork saw the benefits of allowing space for student enquiry, while the importance of a dialogue with students was also evident in Chapter 5, as well as other chapters.
- *Good teaching takes account of the discipline concerned.* Disciplinary considerations are also relevant, a feature of that has been particularly evident in the case studies. In effect we have seen how essential it is for the methods that we employ to align themselves with the values that our discipline holds dear.
- *Good teaching is a collaborative endeavour.* It stems from collaborations between colleagues, as we have seen in every single chapter; and not simply from the individual concerned – we work in a shared environment.

The characteristics of good teaching are also closely aligned with the process of developing your teaching: there is a synergy evident between them. We can say that good teaching involves developing your teaching on an ongoing basis, given the pace of change in higher education and the need to maintain inspiration over the longer term. Continuing professional development, for instance, is now accepted as an integral element of good teaching. However, good teaching also influences the process of developing your teaching: we should develop our practice in a way that recognises the student voice, the demands of our discipline and the experience of our colleagues.

While we evidently need a clear set of aspirations or aims for the development of our teaching, our identity as someone who teaches will comprise far more than this. After all, my personal history will make it more difficult to realise some aspirations than others. In particular, your identity can be expressed in the form of an ongoing story, a narrative about your practice. The following questions provide prompts to help you articulate the story that underpins your teaching:

- What initially drew you to your discipline? What are the values held dear by this discipline? How can you reflect them more fully in your teaching? (You might have been attracted to a discipline simply because you were good at it – but would this sustain your attempts to open it up to others as well?)
- Why did you choose to teach?
- What are the major threads of your life that influence your teaching? Are there any important aspects of your life that have never had an opportunity to affect your teaching? Why not?
- To what extent is your identity rooted in your research? How does the relationship between your research and your teaching influence each other? What synergies can you exploit between these?
- What do you find compelling in your teaching? What is it in your teaching that your students react to with enthusiasm?
- What values underpin your teaching? Are you willing to take risks in order to help your students learn? Or would you rather play safe?

You might think of one or more critical incidents in your teaching that encapsulate your approach, or that help to illuminate each of these above questions, analysing the incidents in light of the advice given in Chapter 4. In Case study 10.1, Denise Batchelor begins to explore her own story by starting with a critical incident in her teaching.

Case study 10.1
HEADING FOR A SHOWDOWN?

The discussion of Donne's sonnets was progressing well, with lively opinions being voiced by the seminar group. In the corner of the classroom stood a tall, dusty four-panelled black screen, abandoned after some past event. Within the enclosure formed by the panels sat X, as he had done for the last five weeks, mostly silent, then suddenly, invisibly and aggressively, stabbing angry and perceptive comments into the air.

The other students found the situation exasperating and amusing. I sensed their longing for me to confront X, insist that he conform, engineer a showdown. As a new and inexperienced lecturer my mind told me this is what a good teacher would do, what I should do. What would happen if the head of department heard that I was allowing a subversive student to lurk behind a screen, potentially sabotaging the smooth running of the class?

Something held me back. In week six X emerged and joined the class. Nothing was said publicly. Privately, X revealed that he had hated school, where he was labelled a failure and expelled for spectacular misbehaviour. He was building up to a similar dramatic scenario again. But something held him back.

Looking back at this nerve-racking incident many years later, I see now that any personal philosophy of teaching I have evolved since was present in embryo then, although as a novice I was acting purely and anxiously on instinct. Remembering this reminds me to try to tread carefully in mentoring staff and working with beginning teachers, to hold back from expressing my own ideas and interpretations too early, and to respect and trust colleagues' developing and different voices as they unpack and reflect on their experiences.

The value implicit in this episode that has become fundamentally important to me in subsequent years of teaching – and, now, researching into the concept of student voice – is respect for students as individuals, seeking to:

- allow students space and freedom to be themselves rather than subscribing to a fixed idea of a student, an inflexible expectation of who and what students should be;
- accept students where they are;
- recognise that vulnerability in students manifests itself in unexpected ways;
- take risks;
- stay open to being surprised;
- have the courage to be myself in my teaching;
- listen to everything in a classroom, silences as well as words, in myself as well as my students.

Denise Batchelor, Business, Computing and Information Management Faculty, London South Bank University

We can ask of each possible development or, indeed, teaching method that we employ, 'How does this fit with my personal story as a teacher or academic?' If an action conflicts with my story, or fails to enhance it, then we might well draw back from taking on the new development, while if it heads in the right direction, we can invest ourselves in it, knowing that it is for this that we are in fact working. We thus see that a personal story can give meaning to your attempts to develop your teaching, as MacIntyre (1984: 216) notes: 'I can only answer the question "What am I to do?" if I can answer the prior question "Of what story or stories do I find myself a part?"'

An important part of our stories are the roles that both we and others play within them, as Denise evidently found. We can take a passive approach to a role that we take on, or engage more actively, as we saw in Chapter 9. All our stories involve other players as well, and their choices affect our choices and, indeed, our own ability to develop, as particularly evident in Chapter 6. Just as the circumstances are given to us, so also the roles of those around us play an important part in shaping our story. You will thus also want to explore whether there are further networks, collaborative contexts or communities of practice in which you can participate more fully, or contexts in which you can take greater responsibility. A mentor, certainly, can help provide access to these networks, as we saw in Chapter 7. When such social situations and roles align closely with your own aspirations and values, then coherence will certainly be added to the way in which you develop your teaching.

You may also find it helpful to move from creating a story to articulating your identity as a teacher in further ways. You might want to develop an action plan for the development of your teaching. Your goals, and the actions associated with them, need to be rooted quite clearly in your history and your present situation. Then, of course, you need to carry it out, reflecting on its usefulness and evaluating its effectiveness. Another option is to write a personal philosophy of teaching, and indeed of your teaching development. This would include attention to your conception of teaching, the methods you employ in teaching and in developing your teaching, and the values and principles that underpin your practice, and its development.

Review point 10.2
A PERSONAL PHILOSOPHY

In order to create a personal philosophy of teaching, or personal philosophy of teaching development, you might reflect on the following:

- What method of teaching or developing your teaching do you rely on most frequently?
- Why do you not use another method?
- What do you think would happen if you changed that method?
- What does this tell you about your attitudes and approach towards student learning?

SINGLENESS OF PURPOSE

A clearly articulated sense of identity as someone who develops their teaching enables a further factor to come into play: the readiness to make choices that align with your vision. We need a singleness of purpose as we seek to develop our teaching, a purpose that aligns with our teaching, our wider academic practice and our lives more broadly, ensuring that we are not blown around by every changing circumstance. As Palmer (1998) argues, it is integrity that enables us to remain true to our own story as an academic. As the pressure on us increases, so does our need for singleness of purpose in holding true to the direction we have chosen to take. The scale of any individual choice, then, matters much less than the direction in which it takes you. Indeed, ongoing small shifts are more likely to enable you to realise your vision of teaching than occasional larger changes, which cannot be sustained.

Stories, action plans, personal philosophies and the roles that we play can all give unity to the way in which we develop our teaching. It is also true that a robust rationale for teaching can stem from these deeper representations of our identity. In both cases, you can then refer your choices back, either explicitly or implicitly, to one of these representations when making decisions. Unless there is a clear connection between your identity and the choices you actually make, any discussion of stories or philosophy will seem utterly indulgent.

This singleness of purpose is also developed through its public manifestation. How can we maintain a commitment to developing our teaching without colleagues finding out about it? We cannot do this on the quiet. We have an obligation to help others develop their teaching, as we realise how much we have gained from others. Dissemination is not simply the icing on the cake but an integral part of this work as the theories of the scholarship of teaching recognise, as evident in Chapter 8.

We will certainly face many choices as to whether and how to develop our teaching; and, indeed, we have tried in this book to widen the choice that is open to you in developing your teaching. Even with this choice, though, we still believe that it is possible to maintain a sense of the direction as you take forward your teaching. Give expression to a personal vision of how to develop your own teaching, and follow it to the end.

REFERENCES

MacIntyre, A. (1984) *After Virtue*, second edition. Notre Dame, IN: University of Notre Dame Press.

Megginson, D. (1994) 'Planned and Emergent Learning'. *Executive Development,* 7, 6, 29–34.

Palmer, P. (1998) *Courage to Teach*. San Francisco, CA: Jossey-Bass.

Index